DITCH THE DRAMA

DITCH THE DRAMA

How To Access God's Promises
of Joy and Freedom No Matter What the World
Throws At You

by

Ginny Priz

WordCrafts

Published by WordCrafts Press
Buffalo, Wyoming 82834
www.wordcrafts.net

This book is dedicated to the woman striving to be more,
do more,
and feel less pain.

There is hope.

TABLE OF CONTENTS

PREFACE

God,
Grant me the serenity to accept the things I cannot change,
courage to change the things I can,
and wisdom to know the difference.

Have you ever thought life seems easier for other people? Have you asked yourself, "Why is life so hard? Why does it have to hurt so bad? Why do so many bad things happen to me? Why do some things have to change? Why do other things *never* change? Why don't they love me? Will I ever be good enough? Why can't I achieve peace? Will I ever be happy?"

These are big questions. These are also natural questions. As we step into new seasons of life and the world around us changes, we've all asked these questions.

I've spent countless hours over my lifetime searching high and low for the "right" answers. At first, I looked to the world with my eyes. I looked to my friends, family, mentors, teachers, therapist, boyfriends, books, movies and TV.

Day and night I wrestled. *Will I ever be good enough?* The questions were on a constant loop. *Why is life so hard?* They took up residence in the back of my mind like a relentless buzzing. *Why do I hurt so bad when every one else has it together?* The harder I tried to answer them, the harder life became. *Why can't I be at peace?* Over time, I relied on alcohol more and more to turn down the volume of the buzzing. *Why don't they love me? Why is life so hard?*

I was working harder and harder to make everyone around me happy. Life was slowly spinning out of control. Panic attacks became a regular occurrence. The tighter I clung to control, the more it slipped through my fingers.

I remember crumpling onto the bathroom floor in tears one night after making my way through most of a bottle of wine. In exhaustion and desperation, I cried out to God.

"Lord! Why doesn't life come with a freaking instruction manual!? People suck! This is too hard! It hurts way too much! I know this isn't what you want for me. And the Bible is great and all, but I need a beginner manual. I need "Insert tab A into slot B" kind of instructions!"

The Lord, rightly so, chose to be silent that night. I was in no fit state to hear His truth in that moment. I am thankful for His grace and patience with me even at my most disrespectful, whiny moments - like that one. Despite my ungrateful attitude and continued resistance, He heard my prayer and answered it.

When I finally put down my pride and sought help for alcohol, my instruction manual for dummies arrived in the form of the Serenity Prayer:

God,
Grant me the serenity to accept the things I cannot change,
courage to change the things I can,
and wisdom to know the difference.
Amen.

One of the really cool things (and really frustrating things) about God, is that He doesn't always announce the gifts He gives us. Sometimes we have to marinate in them for a while before we are able to see their power. That's how the Serenity Prayer worked for me. It wasn't until after I actively used this approach to life for some months that I finally realized this was indeed my instruction manual. It forced me to start addressing the emotions and situations that arose in front of me.

I was finally able to shut down the relentless questions because I finally understood they were *the wrong questions*. It was the questions themselves that kept me stuck. By trying to find out *why* people hurt me or *why* each situation was unfair, I stopped myself from actually accepting the pain and moving on. By asking, *will I ever have peace*, I continued to assume my peace, joy and happiness would always be in the future instead of choosing them in the moment.

I was determined to ditch the drama I had created and carried around in my mind up to that point. I became tireless in applying the Serenity Prayer to all situations, people and emotions in my life. The effect has been astounding.

Where I was once cynical, I am now optimistic. Where I was once terrified, I am now confident. Where I was once self-centered, I now have a desire to help others. The buzz and drama in my mind have been replaced with peace. I am truly a new creation in Christ, set free by God's love.

And, yes, I am aware that sounds like Christian-ese words. But that's just too bad, because it's true. I am free from the fear and despair that haunted me for a decade. Every day I have joy, excitement, satisfaction, gratitude and peace. I have overcome the lies I once believed, and I now walk in truth, unburdened.

I have been set free. My God has set me free.

Some days are harder than others, of course, because this is still life. We can never arrive at serenity. There are too many variables that change daily. Serenity is not a destination – it's a journey. Life is ever changing and the most we can do is make the best decisions we can to keep us along a path of serenity – one day at a time.

Having emerged victoriously from the brutal search for answers, I feel God has called me to share what I have learned. In early 2014 He encouraged me to start writing. In fact, the word He used (over and over) was "write." No matter how I asked Him to clarify, the answer was always that one word, "write."

I began with a blog at ginnypriz.com called "Serenity Journey" in 2014, but soon after, it became abundantly clear a book was the only way I could accurately share, in depth, the freedom that was available.

What follows is that "insert tab A into slot B" instruction manual I wish I'd had much earlier. This is my humble attempt to explain how a close relationship with the Lord, coupled with the Serenity Prayer can give you access to the peace and joy and freedom that scripture describes and promises to believers.

> *"For freedom Christ has set us free; stand firm therefore, and do not submit again to a yoke of slavery."*
>
> Galatians 5:1 (ESV)

> *"Then you will know the truth, and the truth will set you free."*
>
> John 8:32

> *"So if the Son sets you free, you will be free indeed."*
>
> John 8:36

> *"Now may the God of hope fill you with all joy and peace in believing, so that you will abound in hope by the power of the Holy Spirit."*
>
> Romans 15:13 (NASB)

*"These things I have spoken to you so that My joy
may be in you, and that your joy may be made full."*

John 15:11 (NASB)

*"The Lord gives strength to his people; the Lord
blesses his people with peace."*

Psalm 29:11

The promises are true. No matter what is going on in your life, there is hope. Even when surrounded by a darkness that never seems to quit pushing you down, there is hope of a life filled with serenity and satisfaction with the Lord.

INTRODUCTION
Deconstructing Drama

"Peace I leave with you; my peace I give you. I do not give to you as the world gives. Do not let your hearts be troubled and do not be afraid."

John 14:27

Anxiety, fear, worry, anger, conflict, stress, and panic all lead to the same outcome: Drama. For the purposes of this book, I've defined *drama* as any unnecessary conflict, whether it be internal or interpersonal. It is such a little word. Drama; it almost seems harmless. But the reality is, drama has ended relationships, derailed careers, ruined countless hours of sleep, destroyed reputations and started wars. I'm exhausted just thinking of all the destructive possibilities.

I know you can relate all too well, because in some way, shape or form, drama has entered all of our lives. It barrels through suddenly, like a tornado, and leaves everything in its path destroyed or upside down. Whether we caused it, or became an unsuspecting bystander, none of us has escaped the damaging effects of drama.

I'm sure you could point the finger at one or two (or ten) people who have instigated unnecessary conflict. Perhaps, your teenage son who blames you for his pain, your friend who takes advantage of your generosity, your sister who never fails to point out your flaws, your co-worker who gossips incessantly, your in-laws who criticize your parenting, or the passive aggressive bully at work. We rarely lack for sources, do we?

But just because life has the potential for persistent conflict, we do not have to be helpless victims. It is entirely possible to mitigate the destructive impact of drama on your life – you just need to know what to do. None of us will ever be rid of it completely, but we can learn from drama, recognize the warning signs, and nip it in the bud.

Let me hear you say, "Amen!" and "Praise God!" I know you are more than ready to ditch the crazy and pick up more peace and serenity! It might seem impossible in the face of all the world's chaos and vivid emotional wounds, but believe me, all things are possible through Christ. Remember, the apostle Paul sat in a number of jail cells under a death sentence proclaiming joy in Christ. That is radical joy! And that is exactly the kind of freedom that is available to us at every moment.

The practices and principles I teach in this book are the stepping-stones to help you access that freedom. They are powerful if you seriously apply them. Not just for a few days or a week, but consistently. This is a way of life. Jesus modeled it for us, His disciples learned to do the same. You can do this too.

If you've picked up this book, then chances are good you are struggling in this season. I have been there. I know it is painful to be desperate for a quick fix. I know it can feel like the world is chewing you up and you're not sure if you can take it one more day, let alone another month or year.

I am telling you, you will make it. The Lord is walking through this with you. You are not alone. And (unless He sees fit to bless you with a miracle) you will continue to walk out these struggles with Him until you reach that wonderful freedom on the other side.

But, if you want to change your life, *you* have to be willing to do the work. The Bible can guide and inspire you; the Lord will walk with you; I can impart my wisdom and break it down into bite-sized bits. But none of that matters if you are not willing to do life differently.

The first thing you have to do is be willing to get really, unabashedly honest with yourself. If you think that's easy, then let me be the first to congratulate you on being a master of denial.

It is human nature to avoid pain. Either we try to pretend it doesn't exist, or we subconsciously try to distract ourselves. Stuffing or ignoring the issue does not make it go away, however. In fact, it prolongs the pain. Facing uncomfortable truths and processing painful emotions is the only way to ditch the drama in our lives.

It doesn't come easy most times. But it is rewarding. Honesty is the path to freedom, peace, joy and serenity. Like re-modeling your kitchen, sometimes you have to make it worse before you can make it better.

I promise emotions will not swallow you up. They do not have to take over. They are not wrong. They are not shameful. They will not become permanent. In the following chapters you'll learn where they come from and how to walk through them constructively.

Are you saying, "Wait a minute, those ten people are the source of my drama, not me! Why do I have to do the hard work?" Yeah, I've been right there with you. I've blamed everyone from my parents to the travel coffee mug for the problems in my life.

And you might be right that someone or something else

started the conflict. But being right brings pride, not joy; being right does not release you to move on from the conflict, instead it binds you to it. When you take pride in your rightness you show it off like a trophy, but you carry the pain of the conflict on your back as well.

And yes, life would be easier if everyone else would just change. Wouldn't it be wonderful if you had the power to make others change or behave as you see fit? On the other hand, what if they had the power to change you as they saw fit? Not such a great alternative, is it? There is no scenario where controlling others is fair. That is why God gave us free will. The only way He can judge our actions is by making sure they are truly our own.

Blaming others keeps us trapped in the cycle of pain and drama. Blaming others will not help you come to peace with a medical diagnosis, old resentments, or feelings of guilt and shame. Blaming will not stop them from starting arguments, gossiping, bullying, or criticizing.

As you'll see, the only person you can change is yourself. So, that is where we focus our efforts. Is it fair? Maybe not. But it *is* fair that God has made each person responsible only for his or herself.

By keeping our gaze on God's truth and being aware of how we are living that out, our lives come into focus. The joy of who He made us to be and the freedom He offers becomes clear. The drama fades to the background.

Where does drama come from?

Drama was not part of God's original design. He did not create drama and call it good. Drama was not introduced until sin entered the world. In fact, drama is the echoing effects of sin. It is the pain and confusion and injustice that lingers far beyond the initial act of our sin.

Sin is born of our choice to trust in the things of this world rather than trusting the Lord. Both sin and drama first appear in the Garden of Eden immediately after Adam and Eve commit the first sin.

> *"At that moment their eyes were opened, and they suddenly felt shame at their nakedness. So they sewed fig leaves together to cover themselves."*
>
> Genesis 3:7 (NLT)

The initial sin was the eating of the tree of the knowledge of good and evil, which was the only fruit in the garden God had set apart from Adam and Eve. They made a choice to trust the serpent's word that the fruit was acceptable for eating over God's promise that they would surely die. *Immediately* the drama starts.

The first echo of sin is their sudden shame. Rather than trusting that the Lord made them perfectly, they doubted and felt there was something innately wrong with their bodies. They were unable to accept themselves as they were, even though God had called them good! (Sound familiar?)

The next echo of sin is in their desire to fix the situation, even though their nakedness didn't need fixing. They stopped resting in the Lord's plan, they got up and started physically moving to remedy their immediate emotional discomfort.

The next echo of sin, motivated them to isolate. Eve didn't ask Adam for help picking out the right fig leaves to accentuate her eyes. No, they were ashamed and found fig leaves on their own – with out each other and, more importantly, without God - to cover their parts that were different.

This drama – these echoes of sin – occurred within the first few seconds of a single sin. When God appears moments later, Adam and Eve chose to continue the drama by blaming and finger pointing.

The world we live in today is broken and rife with sin. Is it any wonder why it is rife with drama as well?

How does drama work?

We learn from the story of Adam and Eve that our decisions have a bigger impact than we can know. And yet God allows us the free will to make those important decisions. Every day is filled to the brim with choices we have to make. We choose which words to use, friends to keep, opinions to have, and prayers to pray.

When we make choices that are rooted in trusting God's promises, we are going to live in greater peace. On the other hand, when we make fear-motivated choices to satisfy our selfish, immediate needs, we open the door to drama and more sin. If it sounds like I'm saying your peace depends on your performance, well, I am, sort of.

Your part does not require a physical performance, but rather keeping a posture of humility and willingness toward the Lord. He can offer His peace, but you still need to be willing to accept it. You will need to trust in Him and in His word above all else. You'll need to seek His will in all your decisions rather than appeasing those around you. The more you seek the more you'll trust, and the more you trust the more peace you'll experience.

Thankfully, God's love does not depend on our performance of the hand or the heart. He will forgive us no matter how many times we move outside His will to satisfy our own discomfort. He will always be patient as we call "time out" or "do over." He will give us as many chances as we need to adjust our heart's posture.

He asks us to change from the inside out – not the other

way around. Changing outward behavior is like putting a Band-Aid on a gushing wound. It might help a little, but it cannot stop what's inside from pouring out. There must first be a change of the heart. Because when you trust in Him, that gaping wound from which you're pouring blood becomes a source of heavenly light from which pours living water.

He wants your trust and your love more than anything else. More than your capacity for book learning. More than your ability to be right. More than your skill at discerning sin. More than your appearance of goodness. Trust in His promises to help you, strengthen you, purify you, and give you peace that surpasses all understanding.

To me, that sounds a whole lot better than trusting a world full of violence, isolation, exaggeration, lies, gossip, resentments, passive aggression, omission of the truth, running away, cheating, stealing, distractions, obsessive thinking, and idolatry. In that world, your main focus becomes self-preservation. And in that state of mind, you are going to look for a solution - anything that will provide immediate relief.

But when you choose faith, you can have confidence that the Lord will preserve and sustain you. There's no need for desperation when you know you are deeply loved and cared for. You are no longer relying on the next best circumstances to fix your situation. You can rest in the Lord's plan and wait on Him to act or give direction.

Here it is plain and simple:

Doubting God = Drama

Trusting God = Peace

"For only we who believe can enter his rest."

Hebrews 4:3 (NLT)

Years ago, I would not have believed it. I would have thought, "that works for *other* people, but not me. I don't think that's going to help me get out of the hell I've carved out for myself." Friend, believe me, I am *not* talking about a Band-Aid. I am *not* talking about a 30-second pick-me-up. I *am* talking about overwhelming joy and peace and safety no. matter. what.

It exists. It is incredible.

It takes time and it takes dedication. When you are ready to accept it, it will be there for you. In the meantime, give yourself grace for your past – God does. I've seen transformation happen for criminals, murderers, deadbeats, and chronic relapsers. God offers this to everyone. Even you...especially you!

Trusting in the Lord's love and understanding how He values you as His priceless child is the cornerstone you need to have a changed life. After that, you can ditch any kind of drama that comes your way.

How do we get rid of drama?

In order to ditch the drama, it is imperative that we start by growing our relationship with God. We must cling to Him and make Him our focus. Alone we have a tiny toolbox of understanding, but with the Lord we have access to His supernatural toolbox—the same toolbox that helped create the earth, stars, and every creature that ever lived. Our privileges to the box are free of charge. All we need do is ask.

But how exactly do we ask for His tools? By asking for peace? Love? Harmony? Abracadabra!? Open Sesame!? If you are anything like me, you want the shortcut. You want to know, "What are the magic words?"

There is one prayer that has stood out in the last 100 years as a sword and shield against drama – The Serenity

Prayer. Written by Reinhold Niebuhr, a pastor, in the early 1900's, this prayer has gained popularity around the world for troubled souls. The first few stanzas of the prayer are the most widely used and very effective. The full prayer is even more powerful and insightful. Here is the full prayer:

Prayer

God,
Grant me the serenity to accept the things I cannot change,
courage to change the things I can,
and wisdom to know the difference.
Living one day at a time,
enjoying one moment at a time,
accepting hardship as a pathway to peace.
Taking, as Jesus did, this sinful world as it is,
not as I would have it.
Trusting that You will make all things right
if I surrender to Your will;
so that I may be reasonably happy in this life,
and supremely happy with You forever in the next.
Amen.

In his lifetime, Niebuhr did not want to take credit for the prayer. He asserted that he used prayers from other teachers and texts and did not deserve glory for the work. However, his writings are the first time history records the prayer and today, he generally receives the credit.

In the last 50 years, recovery programs have adopted the Serenity Prayer as a kind of mantra. This was not the original intention of the prayer. These groups simply found the "magic words" and use them to open God's toolbox. If the Serenity Prayer can help bring the most hopeless back to sanity, imagine the possibilities for all of God's children.

In this book, I will show you how you can use the principles in the Serenity Prayer to quash drama. I will specifically focus on deconstructing the first three lines of the prayer, but I will also incorporate the wisdom from the full prayer in my analysis.

By studying the prayer closely, you can use it as a roadmap. It can show you where you stand and how you can move forward with the least amount of conflict. It's a universal tool. It can be applied to any situation and any person, at any time, to achieve peace. No exceptions.

Let me show you some real-life examples of the Serenity Prayer principles in action.

I'll start with myself because, well, I know it the best! Actually, even though the conscious discovery of this prayer came only 5 years ago, I've unconsciously used these principles for years from as far back as I can remember.

You see, I wear a prosthetic arm. And I think it's killer awesome! Not that I would use it to kill anyone. That was a joke. Don't get all up in *arms* over a joke, now (see what I did there?). Before you start thinking I'm crazy, let me give you a *hand* deciphering my humor (sorry – I couldn't resist!).

You see, while in my mother's womb, my right arm was not fully formed below the elbow. Doctors do not have an explanation for my restricted growth. There was no disease or chemical interference. They only know that 1 in every 2,000 children will simply not develop a full upper limb. So, in essence, I won the lottery! The doctors might be confused, but I am not. I know why this happened. This was God's design for my life. He made me specifically. Not better or worse than anyone else - just different.

My parents always assured me that I was created perfectly. God had seen to it that I was "knit together in my mother's womb" without blemish. I have never questioned otherwise. I'm extremely grateful for both my arms. I don't feel cheated or sad that I missed out on something. In fact, I'm sorry that everyone can't experience the confidence that I have in God's plan for my life.

Plus, I'm sorry that not everyone can take advantage of the one-arm liners I use to diffuse tension. (Hey, need a hand? I can lend you mine!)

Here's where all the Serenity Prayer principles come in: I've had the good fortune to accept my difference from a very young age. I've changed what I could by focusing my attention to the blessing and capitalizing on the humorous aspects of my situation rather than lamenting my inability to make certain shadow puppets (shadow puppets are over-rated anyway).

In all seriousness though, I've flat out refused to hold any resentment toward God for my body. I do not envy people who have two hands. I am not angry at the world because cars and products are not lefty-friendly. I do not rage at people who ask me to hold something or ask, "What happened to your arm?" What would be the point? It would not change my arm. It would not prevent anyone from being born with a similar condition. Instead, I choose acceptance. (Life's a ton more fun that way!)

I'm not the only one using the principles outside recovery rooms. Take, for example, a young woman named Anna who lost her mother suddenly at the age of eighteen. This was a devastating loss for her. Five years later, she still feels the loss deeply, but she has repeatedly decided to choose the joy of gratitude over the drama of resentment.

Anna puts it this way:

"When I start to miss her and feel sad, I can think, "It's not fair that other people have their mothers. It's not fair that she never got to meet her grandchildren. But, what does that do? It will not make it right by complaining.

"Instead, I choose to think of all the things I loved about her and the beautiful memories. I thank God for every moment I had with her. I thank God that I have memories with her and I knew her well."

Anna has accepted that the loss of her mother will continue to be painfully unfair and she cannot change that. But she has the courage to change her focus. She chooses to enjoy the blessing rather than suffer the injustice.

Ultimately, drama has less to do with our circumstance and more to do with our choices. How we choose to address our emotions, focus our thoughts, and believe in the promises of the Bible determines the amount of frustration and drama we suffer. If you are suffering under the weight of drama, most likely it's your own fault. You may not have chosen your current circumstances, but you have chosen drama. There is a distinct difference.

Before you get offended, I understand you probably

didn't consciously choose more suffering. If you are anything like me, you simply relied on the survival tactics you learned in your formative years (people pleasing, manipulation, passive aggression, demands, tears, etc.). Unfortunately, what brought you peace or kept you safe at the age of three is not the answer as an adult. Life is more complex. Without the tools to understand emotions and healthy coping skills, we're all doomed to wander around unintentionally hurting one another.

If you haven't learned healthy coping skills or if you've unconsciously let past hurts dictate your present reactions, it's not your fault. Please, do not beat yourself up. You cannot be expected to practice that which you have never heard of or do not understand. The practices I'll be describing and the exercises provided will give you an introduction to the healthy coping skills you'll need to be free of drama. Let me give you another example of how this works in real life.

Michelle, a dear friend of mine, was diagnosed with inoperable brain tumors. This is the kind of news that could derail even the most faithful believers. But not Michele! Oh, no! She was determined to lean on God to help her beat these invaders. In fact, she renamed the tumors to "rumors" to show how little power they would have over her health.

I wish I had recorded our conversation when she sat down with me to share her news because I've forgotten the exact words. But I will never forget how I felt. I expected tears or fear and uncertainty at the very least. But I walked away feeling just the opposite.

Her attitude did not allow for fear or sadness, only courageous faith and confidence in the Lord's plan. I left her that evening completely confident and reassured. Surely, the

Holy Spirit was at work bringing comfort, but it was her faith which made it possible.

Here is what she has said about her journey:

"I am definitely learning to think differently and respond to situations & circumstances differently so I don't let stress, anxiety & fear control and consume me like I did before. There is definitely a reason I am on this journey and there has been so much good ... I wouldn't change a thing. I'm so grateful to be learning more and more each day how to truly "Let Go & Let God!" He's really got a great plan for my life and it all works out so much better when I just get out of his way."

Are you starting to see a pattern? Michelle accepted her diagnosis, but she also accepted the sovereignty of God, His plan, and His healing powers. She chose faith, which allowed her the courage to press into each moment rather than get caught in anxiety and fear.

I am not trying to sugar coat a very difficult journey. You should know that some days were physically very painful, others were emotionally draining. For months her blurred vision made it impossible for her to drive or work. Stripping a strong woman of her independence will either leave her desperate for control or ultimately more peaceful by surrendering to the Lord's plan. It's her choice.

Even all throughout our own feelings of fear and frustration, a deeper, simultaneous, unshakable peace is possible with Serenity Prayer principles. The Lord's power is released in our lives when we invite Him to share in our journey. Alone we are weak and confused, clinging to the familiar. But we can do all things through Him who gives us strength (Philippians 4:13).

As I unpack the principles of the Serenity Prayer, here

is what you can expect to learn:

- By trusting who we are according to God, we can find our confidence in an identity that cannot be shaken.
- We'll look at exactly why God can be trusted even though He allows pain and uncomfortable transitions to be a part of our lives.
- You'll learn why the trifecta of serenity, courage, and wisdom from the Lord are particularly powerful for inciting peace in our minds, body, and spirit.
- You'll discover the importance of the grief process and feeling your emotions without judgment or shame. Plus, I'll discuss how to start feeling emotions you have ignored or stuffed.
- Learn to identify what you can and cannot change. Sounds simple, but in reality, spinning our wheels is the most common waste of time and energy on the planet.
- Begin to foster courage through faith, action, and vulnerability.
- Discover how to see a God's-eye view of your circumstances rather than destructively pigeon-holing your perspective.
- Explore 10 Wisdom Practices for making healthy decisions when emotional triggers have hijacked your clarity.

God is a God of peace, a God of joy, a God of gentleness, a God of kindness (Galatians 5:22-23). We know this because these traits are fruits of the Holy Spirit. The Lord promises us we will experience these things when we seek Him first.

Notice the fruits of the Spirit are inward experiences.

Rather than calming the storm around us, He calms the storm within us. And by doing so, we are better able to understand the storm around us and make better decisions to navigate those storms as they come. Remember, even if we have the fruits of the spirit such as peace, joy, gentleness and kindness, we are *not* exempt from chaos, grief, harsh words, and selfishness. This is not a magic spell. This is not a throw away prayer to be repeated and hoped in. It is meant to be put into action by you with God's help. It is meant to be understood through first-hand experience transforming your struggles into joyful moments.

When intentionally put into action, the power of the serenity prayer can be unlocked by anyone—even you.

"But those who trust in the Lord will find new strength. They will soar high on wings like eagles. They will run and not grow weary. They will walk and not faint."

Isaiah 40:31 (NLT)

Prayer

Heavenly Father,
I ask you to guide my journey as I learn and take new steps to experience your deep peace. Help me to be honest with myself (and with you) so that I may experience full healing of my heart. Increase my faith and help me to be willing and teachable according to Your will.
In Jesus' name, Amen.

1

GOD
The Alpha and the Omega

"I am the Alpha and the Omega, the First and the Last, the Beginning and the End."
Revelation 22:13 (NLT)

The Serenity Prayer is a request made directly of God – not our family, or spouse, but our God. Why are we asking God for help? Because of who He is.

Who Is God?

He is our father, our mother, our best friend, our constant companion, our conscience, our life source, our love source. He is the creator who knit together every atom and element in the universe. He is in every sunrise, every sunset, and every cloud in between. He is merciful. He is generous. He is eternal, omniscient, omnipresent, omnipotent, timeless, and glorious.

He is truth. He is love.

Every one of our journeys begins and ends with God. The Lord imagined us specifically and loved each of us so much, He had to breathe us into existence. He spent nine months making sure every detail was perfectly coded into tiny molecules of DNA so we would grow in just the way He wanted.

For the Lord, this journey started much further back.

Before creating you, He did the same for your parents and grandparents, and aunts and uncles, generation before generation. Even before that He created universes, this planet, all of nature and life around this globe. And all of it is a message.

The relationship between dark and light, life and death, pain and love, give us clues to the larger, spiritual picture developing around us. If we are willing to be still and pay attention to these things and the promptings in our soul, the true message of His love is revealed.

All of creation may as well be a big ol' billboard saying: "I love you. – Love, God."

Who better to ask for help from than the creator of the universe who happens to cherish you? He is waiting for the chance to grow a personal relationship with you. Your requests are not a burden to Him; God sees them as an invitation to connect with you. (If you are feeling skeptical because you think God doesn't answer prayers, don't go away! I will address this in the next chapter.)

If you understand nothing else about the Lord, I pray you start to recognize He sees you *with perfect love*.

Feeling God's love with your whole heart and being (and not just knowing it in your brain) is the first step to ditching your drama. It's the 100% necessary foundation of drama-ditching.

Love between people can be loyal and lasting and deep and strong. But human love and human attention is also broken. It is impossible for human love to be 100% selfless. To be human is to be needy for spiritual and emotional healing. Therefore, there will always be a selfish component to human love.

Trying to get that healing from another broken person is like a game of tug of war. Some relationships may be a gentle, half-hearted tug of war, while some spiral into a vicious tug into the mud pit in the middle. Both parties will always need more, and a person cannot give what they do not have.

Our need for love and validation can only be sustained by Him: the one who will constantly give and meet our needs. All other love is less.

A relationship with God is the only one that spiritually and emotionally satisfies. He has no needs. He has everything to give you. He will never try to pull you into the mud pit. He will hold you safe in His hands and provide you with more rope than you could ever ask for.

This is why His love is the foundation of a serenity journey and drama-free life. His love requires nothing in return. He may prompt you to love others or ask you to follow His lead, but His love requires *nothing*. It is truly selfless, freely given, forever with no strings attached. Once that love is felt by your heart, it is (or will be) cherished as a priceless gift far above any flawed love or physical gift this world has to offer.

And that is why we pray and ask for help from the Lord. He has everything to give, and you have nothing to lose.

But you don't have to take my word for it. I'm not the only person who has experienced the love of God throughout thousands of years. Take a look at what these folks have to say.

> *"In the end, what matters is not how good we are, but how good God is. Not how much we love Him but how much He loves us. And God loves us whoever we are, whatever we've done or failed to do, whatever we believe or can't."*
>
> Desmond Tutu

"Whether you understand it or not, God loves you, is present in you, lives in you, dwells in you, calls you, saves you and offers you an understanding and compassion which are like nothing you have ever found in a book or heard in a sermon."

Thomas Merton

"The Christian does not think God will love us because we are good, but that God will make us good because He loves us."

C.S. Lewis

"When you know how much God is in love with you then you can only live your life radiating that love."

Mother Theresa

"I know that when I pray, something wonderful happens. Not just to the person or persons for whom I'm praying, but also something wonderful happens to me. I'm grateful that I'm heard."

Maya Angelou

"Heaven means to be one with God."

Confucius

"God's loving plan to save sinners started with Jesus' death and resurrection. The influence God calls you to have for His Kingdom is very simple: just tell the world what He did for you."

Tony Dungy

"Your steadfast love, O Lord, extends to the heavens, your faithfulness to the clouds."

King David – Psalm 36:5 (ESV)

"I thank God for my handicaps. For through them, I have found myself, my work and my God."

Helen Keller

As you can see, the love of God is a powerful thing when we let it into our hearts rather than simply taking up residence in our heads. When the heart is closed off from the Lord, it is open to the drama of the world.

Drama rises when we value people, things, opinions, power, and comfort above the love of God. When we finally understand the value His love brings to our life, the things of the world lose their shine. We can see them for what they are: broken, tarnished, fleeting, and unsatisfying.

One way we can come in closer relationship with the Lord and understand Him better is to empathize with Him. Empathy is necessary to every healthy relationship. Our relationship with the Lord is no exception. Being omniscient and omnipresent, God has this empathy thing down pat. It is we who need to be intentional about our empathy with God if we are to cultivate a connection.

To empathize with how much God loves us, we need to use another of God's great gifts to us: our imagination. This is really how all empathy starts: in your mind. Conjuring up previous experiences and emotions to help us better feel and understand what someone else might feel.

Exercise: Empathy

Try this empathy exercise to feel God's love:
(Follow the direction one at a time – reading ahead may skew your results.)
Think of a person you love deeply *(They can be alive or dead, parent or child, spouse, or pet. You get the idea.)*
Reflect on all the joyful feelings you have because they came into your life.
Let the gratitude you have for this person rise up in you.
Take a few minutes to really feel this love deeply. Let it fill you. Take your time – there's no rush or time limit.
Really soak up that love and gratitude.
Once you are filled or bursting, take a moment to recognize this is how God feels about you.
Can you imagine God loving you with same kind of intimacy and warmth? If this is difficult, take a moment to imagine Him seeing your heart and loving you for you *(not your past or future, but you.)*
Can you imagine loving yourself with that same full love?
(Actually, that is just a fraction of how God loves you. Even when we are fit to burst, we can only experience a taste of the love God is capable of feeling.)

A printable version of this exercise is available online at:
www.ditchthedrama.net.

Like a parent, God doesn't care what I've done or will do - He loves me still. He never stops for lunch. He doesn't get distracted by war or politics or TV or family. He will reach out to me personally always. Whether I am willing to receive it or not, He continues to send His love to this unworthy human. And that truth brings me to my knees in tears of gratitude.

He is not subject to broken human tendencies. God does not fit in a human box. He does not lie or deceive. He will not turn His back on you or abandon you. He will not hurl insults at you or tell you "you're not good enough."

He walks in step with you at every moment, hears every prayer, sheds every tear with you, feels your fear and anger and sadness. He exists at all times and sees the end.

He wants you to have life to the fullest.

This is important, don't miss this: He wants you to have life to the fullest. That means a life full of peace, and love, and joy, and confidence, and satisfaction; free of drama, resentment, anxiety, and fear. You can trust Him to bring you that life, especially if you trust Him and request His help specifically.

A full life does not mean a path free of conflict or loss. It means a life where the physical cares of this world lose value and the spiritual gifts offered are priceless. It means having the ability to accept the difficult and unexpected. It means relying on God to be with you through every 3 a.m. phone call, embarrassing moment, and harsh word. It means having the courage to walk in His will and fulfill your role in His love story.

A full life means loving with your whole heart, forgiving with every breath, and thanking God for every moment of this unpredictable, messy life. It means freedom from obsessive thoughts and destructive coping skills. It means overcoming your fears with faith, recognizing the uselessness of worry and trusting that God has it all in His hands.

He can be trusted to bring challenges, conflicts, and losses at just the right times and in just the right ways that will allow you to live more fully/freely on the other side of that challenge. All you need do is walk through it with Him.

As long as we keep God in our direct line of site, we can return to peace. As long as we are seeking and learning, we are cultivating our fullest life. Like a sunflower turning to face the sun, we follow where He leads to walk a serenity journey.

This is not to feed His ego. God does not possess the human need of power through your obedience. His needs are met within the trinity. He simply wants you to be in relationship to exchange love with you. It is for our benefit that we follow our Heavenly Father. Because seeking God is the first step to living life to the fullest. And even though He sees our brokenness, He will love us eternally.

That is why we put our requests for serenity, courage, and wisdom at His feet. We cannot ditch drama and navigate our emotions on our own power. We need an anchor we can cling to in times of confusion when all seems lost.

"So God has given both his promise and his oath. These two things are unchangeable because it is impossible for God to lie. Therefore, we who have fled to him for refuge can have great confidence as we hold to the hope that lies before us."

Hebrews 6:18 (NLT)

Prayer

Heavenly Father,
Open my eyes to see you as my loving Abba. Give me ears to hear
the love story contained in Your Word, and give me an open heart
to receive Your love. Cast away any false ideas I've had about
Your character and love so that Your truth can take up residence
in my heart and mind.
In Jesus' name, Amen.

2

GRANT ME
Why can we trust God to provide?

The serenity prayer is a request, plain and simple. It specifically requests gifts from the Holy Spirit: serenity, courage and wisdom.

The reason we can ask for these things is God's grace. His amazing grace!

As sinners we have no right to ask anything of God. He is perfect and our sin nature cannot exist in the same place with such holiness. Like oil and water, some things cannot exist in the same space. It is necessary for us to live separate from the creator, for now.

But the story does not end there. Though we continued to hurt and offend God with our selfishness and pride, God sent His son to die on the cross so the price of our sin - which is death - would be paid by Him and our selfishness would be forgiven completely. Our sins, though they may have physical consequences here on earth, are spiritually washed clean by God's perfect love. That is grace.

Because of these actions, we can ask for anything in Jesus' name and it will be done.

Well, not necessarily. There are exceptions. God will not give us a red velvet cupcake just because we are hungry and we have enough faith. Asking to fulfill our own selfish or earthly desires are not necessarily honored by God.

Yet, if we ask humbly for His assistance in honoring His will, our request will be honored. By asking for serenity to accept His will, courage to do His will, and wisdom to discern His will, we are honoring His kingdom. This kind of prayer will be answered.

Please understand that God does not withhold the desires of our heart out of punishment or anger. He withholds that which is not good for us. A parent would not deny their child vegetables at dinner because they are beneficial for the child. His will is beneficial for us, and He will not withhold it. But when the child tantrums because they want blue crayons for dinner, a parent has to withhold that out of safety for the child rather than anger or punishment. Like children, it is safer for us to rely on the wisdom of the parent.

Even with the power of the Serenity Prayer, it does not follow that His answer to your cries will be easy. It could mean you will have to accept a long wait ahead of you. Most likely, His answer will require you to step outside your comfort zone.

Some of the things God has asked me to accept are His love, others' dislike of me, lost job opportunities, my limitations and failings, other's cruelty, and His forgiveness. Even though God's love and forgiveness sounds lovely, these were still difficult for me to accept and took me well out of my comfort zone.

Finding my limitations and saying "no" to friends was extremely uncomfortable for me, at first. The codependent, people pleaser inside of me was terrified of rejection. It was physically painful to back out of a commitment because I felt overextended. My stomach was queasy and my shoulders were tense with knots.

But the more I honored my limitations and practiced those boundaries, the more I realized my fears were unfounded. I slept better knowing I wasn't running myself into the ground for affection.

Have you ever complained about how your prayers were answered? I know I have. We want the easy way – the miracle. Alas, we are rarely shown the easy way. Not because we are being punished. Not because we are being abandoned. But because the journey teaches us far more effectively than the miracle. The journey matures us. Our maturity makes us more effective at loving others, teaching others, and living fully.

Do not be discouraged when your challenges do not disappear with prayer. Instead, rejoice. He gives us challenges to teach us a better way to live. The miracle could make life easier in the moment, but we'd be left with the same weaknesses and bad habits.

"Give a man a fish, and he will be hungry again tomorrow; teach him to catch a fish, and he will be richer all his life."

M. Loane

"Consider it pure joy, my brothers and sisters, whenever you face trials of many kinds, because you know that the testing of your faith produces perseverance. Let perseverance finish its work so that you may be mature and complete, not lacking anything."

James 1:2-4

The challenge God presents us is not drama. Rather our

resistance to walk forward into His teaching is the drama we create. The longer we avoid, ignore, and resist the path God has asked us to follow, the more discontent we become. There is a restlessness and uneasiness that emerges as a result of our fear. Stepping forward into His will is ultimately what brings us peace.

Remember, these challenges are not to punish you, but to strengthen you. Acceptance requires mourning; change requires uncertainty and lack of control; wisdom requires vulnerability and humility. Blessings are often brought to us through struggles that grow our faith and trust in God. If we pay attention, we see God is simultaneously revealing His heart for us in the way He guides us toward more freedom and satisfaction.

Prayer

Heavenly Father,

I am humbled by Your generosity in laying down the life of Jesus so that we might never be separated. Help me to honor such a gift by appreciating the challenges You have set before me as gifts themselves.

Guide my steps to walk in Your will. Remind me to pray without ceasing so that we may grow ever closer.

In Jesus' name, Amen.

3

THE SERENITY
What does it mean to surrender?

Serenity literally means tranquil and peaceful. By this definition, serenity can be created by sitting in a quiet room with the lights dimmed. But you and I know that internal struggle cannot be made peaceful by external ambience. No matter our surroundings, internally, there can still be a lot of unrest.

We can try to fight anxiety with distractions, pills, exercise, breathing exercises, TV/movies, or setting more goals. We can fight to control our situation, fight to control our loved ones, fight to control the outcome of our struggle. Unfortunately, these are all losing battles.

Serenity cannot be fought for or won. Serenity can only be gained by surrender.

What is Full Surrender?

> *"Stop your fighting - and know that I am God,*
> *exalted among the nations, exalted on the earth."*
> Psalm 46:10 (HCSB)

Internal serenity is created by releasing what you want in the moment and trusting in God's long-term plan instead. When we surrender to God there is relief. We drop the struggle for our agenda and allow God to do the work of deciding the best outcome.

This does not mean we become heartless and give up caring. We continue to care about the outcome and hope for the best. Instead, we give up wishing and striving for our will.

Full surrender means giving up our desire to change what is outside of our control.

We surrender our worries of what the future will bring because we recognize that our "what ifs" will only change the future by diminishing our ability to be present.

We surrender the past and the injustice we feel has been done, because loathing the past diminishes our ability to love in the present moment.

We surrender other's opinions. When we consider our value is priceless simply because we were created by the Lord, we can more easily see the validation of others will never satisfy or sustain us.

We surrender our journey because His plan is better. Just as God created you specifically, He had a unique journey in mind for you. He has closed doors and made opportunities available to bring you the right people and to the right places at the right times. Our sphere of influence in this moment is the canvass God has given us to create love, reveal truth, receive His teaching, and experience Him. We are exactly where God wants us.

If we cannot surrender these things, the drama creeps up. We begin thinking in circles about a conflict without reaching a conclusion; obsessively turning it over in our minds hoping to make it right somehow. We experience intense emotional reactions to small, unrelated problems. We cling to our need to be right and excuse our actions because our intentions were good. Our friends and family become frustrated and begin to point out our negativity, anger, need to be right, and/or control issues. Eventually, our decision-making suffers from our selfish thinking and others are hurt.

I wish there were a magic formula to remove our personal will, so our struggles could easily disappear. But then, that would cheapen the experience. Our God is a personal God who meets us right where we are. He will help each of us surrender in personal ways only we can understand. And those experiences are infinitely more meaningful *because* they are private, personal gifts.

He doesn't want a relationship that is mass-produced and cookie cutter. He is passionate about you and knows the unique lens through which you see the world. The more time you spend seeking His will in a posture of surrender, the more you will come to know and understand God's personal language with you. He will reveal truth to your heart that can only be seen through your individual lens. Such is His love for you.

In moments when I feel *completely* surrendered to the Lord, my mind clears of everyday worries and I find myself listening with my whole being. The world and the people in it fade into the background. My muscles relax. My breathing is deeper. My soul feels translucent somehow; as if He and I are vibrating in the same rhythm, occupying the same space. Perhaps this is what is Jesus meant by "you are in Me, and I am in you." (John 14:20)

Unfortunately, surrender is not a one-time event. It is a daily and sometimes hourly decision to put down our desires. As you learn your personal love language with the Lord, there are some practical steps that can help you in your path to surrender.

Remember that God is good and trustworthy.

Although God cannot be trusted to shield you completely from pain, He can be trusted to mold you and shape your life in a way that is satisfying and meaningful beyond what you can presently imagine.

He does not shield you from all fear and pain because that is how we learn and grow.

There are plenty of Bible stories illustrating the concept of useful pain. Just look up Joseph and Moses and David and Jesus. This theme is used repeatedly to remind us that God often brings us to situations that seem impossible only to use them to catapult us further on our faith journey.

I remember in 2010 while organizing my move from New Jersey to Tennessee being nervous about income. I knew God had called me to live in Tennessee, but I did not have a job set up for my arrival. As the time drew closer to leave, God prompted me to share my resignation with my boss a full four weeks earlier than I'd planned. It was a risk. I could have been fired on the spot.

I prayed all morning before our meeting and called on God's strength and peace. I went into that meeting terrified. I was going against every people pleasing bone in my body. I wanted to cut and run as soon as possible with as little confrontation as possible. And yet here I was creating an opportunity for the standard two-week torment to last three times as long.

What came out of my obedience was a job. Because I followed His prompting, we had time to work out a scenario where I was able to keep my job and work from my new home in Tennessee. A position I continued to fill full-time for another four and a half years.

That was the first time I remember getting on my knees to thank God. For me, this was a miracle. Deciding to leave everything and everyone I loved was hard. Knowing I would have a job was proof that He would take care of me, even when I couldn't see it coming.

What about your own life? Has there been a time in your story when circumstances seemed impossible, but God taught you more about His character instead? Maybe God created an opportunity you never expected? This is one of the ways He shows He can be trusted to love and care for us. Collect these stories and treasure them. They are His personal miracles for you.

At moments when you are feeling the pressure of an "impossible" situation, look back through these miracles and remind yourself that God has always come through (whether you realized it immediately or years later).

Remembering His works this way, is actually a Biblical practice. At important moments in the Israelite's lives they would erect altars or pile stones to remind them of God's provision in their lives for generations. Before the Israelites entered the Promised Land, God required that the law of Moses – including the story of the Israelite's miraculous freedom from Egypt – be read every seven years to the people. This was to be a regular reminder to the Israelites of the power and character of the God to whom they belonged.

We are no different than the Israelites needing constant reminding of God's character and intentions. Let's face it, as humans, we have short-term memories. And the presence of the enemy stalking around the earth working to lead us astray is constantly chipping away at our armor. Reminding ourselves of God's trustworthy character is necessary to prevent the warping of our faith.

We need reality checks to keep us on track. To easily and consistently surrender to the one who loves us, we need to be reminded of His loving, personal acts.

Slow down.

Filling every minute of the day with activity, people, work, travel, family and social media is a sure way to pick up the kind of momentum that takes us further away from serenity.

Popular opinion would have you believe you are useless if you are not busy "doing." And that makes it especially easy to get caught up in the comparison game. Believe me, you are not inadequate if you haven't accomplished in one month what your friend has accomplished in one morning.

Our busyness will not make us more important nor more valuable. But faced with that comparison, your brain is primed to start generating those familiar lies:

- *You'll never be successful because you can't keep up with other people.*
- *Just give up now; you don't have what it takes.*
- *Leave this project to someone else. They will do it better than you, anyway.*
- *What have you done for God that comes close to that?*
- *You haven't made a significant impact on the world, so you are useless.*

These are all lies designed by the enemy to push a false, works-based, worthiness system. In God's kingdom there are no systems. His love is freely given. All His children are important for their own reasons. The eye cannot perform the function of the spleen. Each has a different role – none less worthy than the next.

If we stay in our busyness and never slow down enough to remember the truth of God's promises, it becomes harder and harder to fight the momentum of the world's influence. And those lies will sweep you up into a frenzy of drama before you even knew there was a breeze coming. We don't need busyness to be successful (in society or in God's kingdom), we need balance. We need quiet and active listening to the Holy Spirit just as we need activity and people.

The world will not fall apart if we stop pushing and start resting in Him. We were never meant to face this life journey alone. The Lord wants to bear the bulk of our burdens. He wants to shield us from predators by gathering us under His wing.

The more we fight for our own will, the more impossible it becomes for the Lord to fight our battles and shield us from harm.

Take an objective view of difficult situations.

Drama will undoubtedly arise when we start assigning "right" and "wrong" labels or "victim" and "villain" roles to our situations. These types of classifications only serve to separate us from others instead of drawing us closer in love.

Labels help us assign blame, disconnect, and over-simplify. They distance us from the complex truth in favor of the easier answer. Life is not a cartoon movie with clear heroes and villains. We all have strengths and weaknesses. We all have had different experiences that shape our opinions and views of the world.

Active surrender does not mean ridding your life of complex thoughts or emotions. Seeing situations as they are may be complex and uncomfortable, but recognizing truth is the first step toward preventing drama. By labeling and separating yourself from others you are imposing your will onto your situation and ultimately creating drama. Taking an objective stance (as best you can), is an attempt to observe the truth of what is happening – without labels. Remove your emotions from the equation. For a moment, ignore the possible consequences of the situation on your future. Surrender the fight inside and simply observe what has happened around you and within you.

I know all too well this can be difficult. Our need to be right and our need to be blameless is a powerful thing. In fact, these are just other words for the deadliest of sins: pride. Humility allows us to see truth.

Fear tends to skew our vision as well. Fear of rejection or fear of being found out as a fraud or a sinner can keep us in denial for a long time.

This is when it is most important to remember that whatever you discover in your objective observations, God's immense love for you will never change. Whatever you discover in the truth of your situation, God already knows. He loves you still.

There is more drama to be feared from failing to recognize the truth than anything within the truth itself.

> *"No power in the sky above or in the earth below—indeed, nothing in all creation will ever be able to separate us from the love of God that is revealed in Christ Jesus our Lord."*
>
> Romans 8:39 (NLT)

There is more good news. Seeing our lives and interactions objectively is a skill that can be practiced. It can get easier with experience. Plus, it doesn't have to be entirely on our own shoulders. We can seek the counsel of others, who are not as emotionally invested in our situation, to provide an objective view.

Seek Wise Counsel.

"Confess your sins to each other and pray for each other so that you may be healed."

James 5:16 (NLT)

Seeking counsel is not weakness. There is strength in numbers. But do take care in choosing whom you trust for counsel. Whether they are a peer, a mentor, or a pastor, they should have Godly fruit in their lives you can see. Look for evidence of their undeniable commitment to loving others and loving God in their life.

Also, be careful when seeking wisdom that your personal motivations are in the right place. Many times it can be veiled in an attempt to complain, or gossip, or receive validation of our victimization. This kind of behavior only nurtures drama. Examine your heart and make sure that your desire is to humbly seek clarity before involving a third party.

As long as you are fully honest about the situation (and not conveniently leaving out your personal shortcomings), a third party will see the situation more clearly because personal history, desires and fears are not blocking their view. Without a personal investment, they can think clearly and objectively.

God designed us to live in community, and sometimes community is what we need to get better perspective. In isolation, it is much easier to rationalize and ignore our faults. But we cannot deny what our community reflects back at us.

Let go. Stop fighting. Give up control to the one who can be trusted. Surrender and discover serenity.

Prayer

Heavenly Father,
I surrender my will to You today and all the days of my life. Help
me to renew my surrender every day. Instill in me a renewed and
stronger faith in Your promises. As I walk through each day, slow
my pace so that I never move ahead of You.
In Jesus' name, Amen.

4

TO ACCEPT
The steps to acceptance.

The five most stressful transitions you can undergo are moving, loss of job, loss of a loved one, loss of health, and divorce. What causes this stress is not just the physical endurance one must have, but more importantly the emotional resilience to accept such disruptions.

In such drastic circumstances of loss, we are taught the 5 Steps of Grief are necessary to reach acceptance of the loss. But did you know that these steps apply to all forms of loss, even the minor and the imagined?

The path from Denial to Acceptance comes in 5 steps. Denial, Anger, Bargaining, Depression and finally Acceptance.

The Grieving Process.

The speed at which we travel through the grief process and reach acceptance depends primarily on two things: 1) the strength of our attachment 2) our willingness to feel our feelings at each step.

If we are not particularly attached to what we've lost, the process goes smoothly and quickly. For example, if you are frustrated with your current vehicle because it's out of style, needs a new muffler system, and the air conditioning hasn't worked in 2 years, you won't have difficulty moving through the grief process when someone totals your vehicle and your insurance company gives you a check for a fully functioning version of your car.

On the other hand, if you just purchased your dream vehicle – a rare classic car – and it is totaled in the same accident, you will most likely spend a longer time going through the grief process and feel those emotions more deeply.

No matter the transition in our life, there will be some level of grief that accompanies the change. It's completely natural. It is also absolutely necessary to work the steps of grief if we are to experience life to the fullest.

Recognizing emotions is the first step. Even just acknowledging them to yourself can be a major victory.

Denial is a very natural response, especially if you have spent any amount of time hiding or stuffing your emotions. Denial is a knee-jerk reaction built into our psyche as a kind of protection from feeling intense emotions. It is meant to be a temporary state.

When we hold on to denial and stay there, drama is never too far behind. Our actions and thoughts are not on the same page. Our actions may move ahead while our emotions are stalled. For example, when children leave for college, life changes dramatically for parents. Mom or Dad may work late or take on more responsibility to pretend everything is fine when they are really using work to mask their loneliness and confusion about their new stage of life.

Avoiding those emotions leaves us more vulnerable than we realize. By getting stuck, we can experience increased emotional outbursts, raised blood pressure, feelings of anxiety, difficulty concentrating, and strained relationships.

The full surrender I talked about in the last chapter is

what helps us to deal with our first grief step – denial. If we are quiet, surrender our will, and try viewing life objectively we should be serene enough to emerge from denial. From there on out, the process takes on a life of it's own.

After denial, the other steps – anger, bargaining, depression, and acceptance – are rarely laid out in a clean, straight line. They are more likely to be a jumbled mess, sometimes repeating again and again. High intensity of emotions can come at every step, or maybe just one of the steps. You can travel through them almost instantly, or it may take years. There is no right way to grieve, except to keep traveling through as best your can.

It is this unpredictability and intense discomfort of grief emotions that makes this uncomfortable process even more difficult. We are hardwired to avoid pain. The fight or flight responses are opposite, but they are both the shortest distance to resolution of the conflict. Fighting will determine a winner relatively quickly while flight will remove us from the immediate threat.

There is a child's book/game called "Going on a Bear Hunt." Do you know it? I played this growing up and I loved it. The poem describes a hunter searching the wilderness for a bear (In the game, you act out the motions). And each time the hunter is faced with an obstacle (a river, field of reeds, a mountain, etc.) the hunter proclaims he "can't go over it, can't go under it, can't go around it, gotta go through it." And that's really how we need to approach the grief process. Straight through it.

Acknowledging emotions is scary because it means we have to experience them. It takes courage to face the unknown. But emotions are temporary as long as we feel them.

The Latin word for emotion is *emovere*. It means to

remove or to move out. Feeling our emotions is actually moving them out of our body and mind. Holding on to them is when the problems arise.

One summer in my mid-twenties, I went "down the Jersey shore" for a long weekend with two of my best girlfriends – Joy and Lisa (whose names have been changed to protect the innocent). It was a rough season for all of us, for our own reasons. The weekend started out rocky.

Joy was late and cranky after sitting in traffic. She was vocal about not wanting to be there because her grandmother was ill and would rather be with her. Lisa wanted to distract herself from loneliness because her daughter's father was getting married to another woman. I, myself, was still hurting from a sudden break up a few weeks earlier and wanted to forget that I was living with my parents while looking for a new apartment.

The first night we bickered about the smallest things – where to eat, who should drive, and which iPod was to be played. This was not our typical behavior, but we were all hurting and all trying to run away from our grief in some way. We all wanted a fun, exciting weekend as planned, but our hurts were getting in the way.

Over the next few days, we each took turns having our own personal crying sessions. Joy went first, then Lisa. And after each moment of vulnerability, we laughed and bickered a little less. I was the last to let my walls down.

I suppose I thought my pain shouldn't be recognized because my friends' struggles were more fresh. I didn't want to dishonor their pain by making our time about me. The plan, all along, was to help them.

At the time, I thought avoiding a melt down was the best thing to do, never realizing my mind was so consumed with stuffing my own pain that my own pain was all I could focus on. I found a way to bring every conversation back to my achy heart, my housing struggle, me, me, me. In trying to avoid my emotions, I smothered everyone in them.

Then, on the second evening, as much as I tried, I couldn't hold back my emotions any longer. I sat on the hotel bed and tears streamed down my face. Lisa saw me and came over. I apologized, but I just couldn't stop. She sat with me for a while with Joy and they let me cry.

Lisa gave me a gift that day. She validated my emotions. Even after I had failed to empathize with her all weekend, she showed me love. I'm not sure if she understood she was modeling God's grace in that moment. It healed a piece of me though, just the same.

The bickering…well, I won't say it stopped completely, but it was softer. The bite had gone out of our bark. And after all that vulnerability, we were closer friends than when we had arrived. And we all felt lighter. The world was better because we could move those emotions up and out.

It is a natural reaction to be scared to deal with intense emotions. But we have to make a choice at every step. We can choose to hold on to the negative emotions of the grief or we can walk through them and clear out space for love and joy.

Remember, the pain is not meaningless. These are growing pains. We grow in knowledge, people skills and emotional skills each time we feel pain. Rather than suffering at the hands of our emotions, we are intentionally moving forward in our life and growing our capacity for peace and serenity.

Grieving Imagined Loss.

One of the Lord's greatest gifts to us is imagination. It

is perhaps simultaneously the most powerful and the most overlooked of His gifts. That is why it is so important that we use this gift wisely.

Creating expectations for our future can be helpful in establishing structure in our lives - making order in the chaos. But forming strong attachments to our expectations only sets us up for a harder grief process when those expectations are not met.

Expectations create an imagined future we consider belongs to us – whether the expected outcome is good or bad. When reality makes that expectation impossible, we have no choice but to grieve what we imagined was once ours. Even if it only existed in our own imagination, for us, it was real; for us, it was ours.

Anxiety.

Anxiety will most likely become a part of your grief process. But there is a reason anxiety does not get its own step in the cycle: anxiety is not a true emotion.

The term "anxiety" describes a series of symptoms that occur when we attempt to deny or ignore negative feelings of fear, guilt or shame. Shallow breathing, racing heartbeat, tense muscles, inability to concentrate, desire to withdraw, and cyclical thinking are all the result of failing to address your emotions.

The only way to remove anxiety is to acknowledge the emotions you are avoiding and then feel them to release them. This can be scary for a lot of folks.

When I first started learning to feel my emotions, there were a number of popular lies and false beliefs I had to dispel.

Maybe you can relate to some of these?

Lie #1: No one knows how this feels.

If you attend any support group ever, you'll realize just how similar we all are. And just how similar our struggles really are. You are not alone; you just haven't shared your struggles with the right person (or anyone!).

Lie #2: No one cares about how I feel.

God and Jesus and the Holy Spirit care deeply. And, as I go through the writing process, I am praying for you – every single person who reads this book – I have loved on you through prayer! So, no excuses, there at least 4 of us who love you and care about your struggle.

Lie #3: I put myself in this mess, now I need to clean it up on my own.

We created this mess on earth. Adam and Eve helped us all fall. But Jesus died for us on the cross while we were still sinners in this mess. The whole point of the 10 Commandments and the Sermon on the Mount was to help us recognize we can't do this life alone. It is impossible for us as broken beings. We need help. We need God. We need Jesus. Accept His help.

Lie #4: I should instinctually know how to handle emotions.

Just because we are born with the ability to experience emotions, does not mean we are instinctually equipped to manage them. Emotional skills are taught and caught as children in our nuclear family first. Broken people teaching broken people does not a perfect plan make. We need to go to technical school to learn HVAC systems, and we need emotional education to learn the healthy ways to deal with them. Both are learned skills.

Lie #5: If I start feeling my pain, I will be vulnerable and I will always be vulnerable and in pain.

We feel emotions to release them. You would never say "if I feel happy today, then I will always feel happy." We definitely know that doesn't work. So why would it work the other way around?

Lie #6: I'm a Christian, so I should never be angry.

Even God and Jesus have been angry. Granted, it was righteous anger at those who worked to separate people from the love of God. But they still felt anger when someone attacked their ability to love. Isn't that what you get angry about as well? When someone takes away something or someone you love or enjoy?

Lie #7: Anger is a sin I should be ashamed of.

Anger is the second step in the grief cycle. It is natural. It is healthy as long as we feel it and move through it. We need to be aware of what we do with the anger and how we react to that anger. God has called us to love. Lashing out at others in anger is the opposite of acting in love, and therefore something we want to avoid. The good news is, acknowledging the anger is the first step to managing it.

Lie #8: I should be happy like everyone else.

Everyone else is not happy. Everyone else is not emotionally healthy. Some folks are really great at putting on masks. Some people feel more than others. We all come with different genes and experiences and caffeine levels! Comparing yourself to others is not fair to you, or to them. You cannot tell an apple to be orange just as you could not tell me to be right handed. Our emotional intelligence and skills are similarly incomparable.

The opposite of anxiety is awareness. We have to examine the world inside and outside of our head. It is the fundamental skill you'll need to learn for complete enjoyment of life. Get to know your thoughts, thought patterns, and triggers. It's *your* head. If you don't understand it, who will?

Keeping your mind a mystery keeps you guessing at what will make you healthy. Intentionally discover what you need and then chase after that. Otherwise, you will leave your life to chance.

Shortly after graduating high school I visited Six Flags Great Adventure with a group of friends. It was to be our last visit to the theme park before going off to college. I wanted to have as much time with them as possible and I pushed myself to keep up and ride every ride and stand in every line with them.

Now, I have always been scared of heights. That made rollercoasters a far cry from my comfort zone. Every year I had sat out of at least a few rollercoasters, but this year, I was determined to have as much fun as I could. In my mind, that meant riding all the coasters with my friends because that's exactly what they wanted to do.

As the day wore on, I was feeling more and more anxious. My heart rate sped up, it was harder to stand in line. But I ignored my fear and told myself I was having fun. I pushed through until the end of the day when we had one more rollercoaster to go: *The Viper*.

There was no terrifyingly slow rise to the top of the first hill on this one. But when I sat in the chair and tried to pull down the safety harness to strap me in, something in me broke. My anxiety rose too high. I couldn't do it. I felt claustrophobic and I thought my heart would beat out of my chest.

Instead of securing the harness I got out of the seat and off of the ride. While my friends rode the Viper and had fun, I was trying to calm down and take deep breaths. It must be the stress of leaving home for college, I thought. But I had ignored my fear all day long. I was pushing myself to the limits in the name of "fun." Fun that I wasn't having.

You see how trial and error is a poor tool for your peace and satisfaction? I needed to ride only half of those coasters and I would have gone home happy rather than discovering what a panic attack feels like for the first time.

Embracing Emotional Awareness.

You have the opportunity to have life to the fullest, without drama. Jesus wants you to have it. The Holy Spirit helps you to have it. For your part, you need to stay aware and accept your feelings may be different from what others think they "should be."

I particularly love the Message version of the Bible's translation of 2 Corinthians 10:5:

> *"We use our powerful God-tools for smashing warped philosophies, tearing down barriers erected against the truth of God, fitting every loose thought and emotion and impulse into the structure of life shaped by Christ."*

In this verse we can see how important it is to take every thought captive. If we cannot acknowledge our thoughts, we cannot work to replace the lies with God's true promises. Meditation, prayer, taking the time to really listen, journal, and explore your own thoughts and feelings are all imperatives to peace.

When feeling scared or guilty or ashamed our instinct is to pull back from others in order to hide these emotions completely. Stuffing them down and pretending they are not there is a far cry from healthy living. They do not disappear. They reappear in new ways - often unexpected or unconscious ways - and at inappropriate times.

I spent a good portion of my life hiding my emotions because they scared me. I believed that anger was bad – especially because I was a Christian. I truly believed I had to love everyone all of the time and never be angry. So to be a "good girl" I hid as much anger as I possibly could. (The only exception was toward my parents as a teenager and young adult. I'd say I was guilty of letting my emotions fly at them full force on many occasions. Sorry Mom and Dad!)

Basically, I was ashamed of my anger and fear because I equated anger with abandonment. I believed outright anger, would push everyone away. I was terrified that my friends and teachers and coworkers would discover my true feelings. So I stuffed it down much like I did at Six Flags Great Adventure.

Now I understand that anger is a mask for fear, a natural byproduct of the fear emotion. When you are angry, ask yourself – "what am I really afraid of?" This will keep your anger from creating more excessive conflict for you and the people around you.

I was so good at hiding my emotions, eventually I hid them from myself. The anger and fear I wouldn't allow myself to face began to come out in different ways. I was a pressure cooker well beyond maximum capacity trying to keep the lid on my anger.

But it always found ways of escaping: Passive aggressive comments, high blood pressure, panic attacks, binge drinking, and sudden outbursts of misplaced rage quickly followed by deep shame.

Hiding or stuffing emotions is essentially a form of denial – the opposite of acceptance.

A very wise woman once told me that emotions are nothing to be ashamed of. She spoke truth that day. I am sorry to admit I did not believe her at first. It took many years and a paid therapist to finally understand *why* emotions cannot be "wrong." I hope you will learn from my mistake.

Quite simply, emotions are a symptom. Negative emotions are a specific symptom, giving you fair warning you are caught in the grief cycle. Being ashamed of your emotions would be like being ashamed that you have a 102-degree fever. The fever is a symptom of an attack on your body. Hiding the symptom or ignoring it will only hurt yourself and infect others you come into contact with. Like an infectious disease, negative emotions can spread and become increasingly more potent until your ability to live a joyful life is severely threatened.

If you are open to learning from the pain in the grief cycle, you will find you have grown your courage and strength and faith in God when you come out the other side.

I know this can be very hard. But your emotions do not have to rule your life. By ignoring them, they will guide your path more than you realize. Recognizing them, feeling them and letting them go releases you from the emotional prison you created. You set yourself free – this time wiser and stronger.

The journey through the grief takes great courage. It is a brave thing to look at the truth, feel the truth and let it impact your journey. Each time you are successful you will feel empowered, courageous, and free from anxiety.

Remember, as you walk through a painful experience you are not alone. God is walking with you through the mess. You can count on Him to never leave your side so that you can be comforted and still learn a lesson from the pain.

Holding on to that grief and anxiety keeps you in the role of the victim with no one to blame but yourself. There could most certainly be an aggressive person that caused this grief cycle. In the moment of their offensive behavior, you are indeed their victim. But in the weeks, months, and years afterward you become the aggressor against your own life; by letting your emotions dictate your life, you are essentially victimizing yourself. You are choosing to keep yourself in the victim mentality.

Defusing Your Emotions.

I partly feared my emotions because of the erratic behavior I exhibited when intense emotions escaped the dark places of my mind. I hurt people – physically and emotionally. And that caused me deeper shame about my feelings and inability to control them.

What I didn't realize was that I created the pressure cooker and the resulting holes by refusing to acknowledge them in the first place. If I had seen the pressure rising early, I could have easily opened the lid and removed the excess contents before there was a need to plug any holes.

If you are in a season in your journey where you have hit a crisis – that is, what you have done in the past is no longer working and you are searching for a better way to approach this situation – the pressure cooker may need emptying more often than usual. That's why people in crisis will lash out far beyond what a conflict may call for. The pressure is growing and needs to escape wherever it can.

If you are not used to emptying the pressure cooker by feeling your emotions, you might be scared the release will take over completely. I want to reassure you that you are not your emotions. Remember your emotions are symptoms. Intense negative emotions often are symptoms of a bigger problem. They show us where our thinking and God's reality are not matching up.

Therefore, when you finally allow yourself to feel those emotions, you do not have to be a slave to them. You do not have to carry them with you. You are feeling symptoms so you can get to the root of the bigger problem – the lies in your thinking.

When our thoughts are aligned with God's truth we realize we are loved and accepted, created perfectly, forgiven eternally, loved unconditionally, generously blessed, and never forgotten by the only person that matters: The God of the universe. No matter what we have done or people have said, our God sees our heart and does all of this in spite of our flaws.

My parents instilled in me from a young age the importance of keeping my commitments. If I said I would be somewhere, I would be there unless I was highly contagious; no excuses. It is a good work ethic to have, for sure. But some days, that is a high standard to keep, especially if you have spread yourself thin.

Unfortunately, I held myself and my friends to this standard legalistically. I took it as a personal rejection if a friend changed their plans or bailed. And because I was so bad at recognizing my thoughts, I just got angry at my friends. Some days I was better at hiding my anger than others.

Once I realized God would never bail and never reject

me or break plans, I needed less validation through the attention of my friends. I relaxed my stringent requirements on commitments and even gave myself some grace when I was stretched too thin and stopped beating myself up when I was too tired to go out.

In this way and countless others, living from the knowledge of God's promises is freedom. Living from any other belief creates fear, anxiety, and drama.

Grieving brings attention to the problem so we can be healed from the lies and live more freely.

When I hold tight to the lies and false beliefs rather than God's truth, I can feel the pressure building. That's when I like to look under the lid in a quiet and private place where I will not be interrupted.

"But when you pray, go into your room, close the door and pray to your Father, who is unseen."
Matthew 6:6

I enter into prayer and ask the Holy Spirit to help guide me in this undertaking. Then, I relax my muscles and take some deep breaths and remind myself that my emotions do not need to control my behavior – they are not a fundamental part of me. Then, I give myself permission to start feeling.

Exercise: Feel Your Emotions

Get in a safe, quiet place where you will not be disturbed for at least 20 minutes. Take several deep breaths and get into a comfortable position.

Prayer

Heavenly Father,
I know You see all of me and love me still. Thank You for loving me despite my flaws and sins. Help me to bring my thoughts and emotions into the light so You may heal me from the pain I am trying to hide. I ask that You silence any self-depreciating thoughts that arise as I examine my emotions. Place Your peace on me. Allow me to accept my emotions without judgment. Open my eyes so that I might see myself as You see me.
In Jesus' name I pray, Amen.

Continue to breathe deeply. Imagine the tension in your muscles being exhaled with each breath.

With your eyes closed, pay attention to how your body feels. Notice your head and neck, your shoulders, chest, arms, back, stomach, hips, legs, feet. Relax each muscle group as best you can.

Before you move ahead, remember, you are in a safe place and emotions are a symptom. They are something you have and not a permanent part of you.

Once you are relaxed, consciously allow an emotion to rise up to the surface. Imagine you are holding it in your hand.

Examine how it feels and where you feel it in your body.

Just observe, knowing it will not overpower you. If you want to cry, go ahead and cry. If you want to scream or smash something I suggest you imagine doing so in your mind. As uncomfortable as the emotion may be, take some time to sit with it (continue deep breathing) and monitor its intensity. As you feel it without judgment, you'll find the less intense it becomes.

Can you identify the emotion you are feeling? Do you know where and when it came from?

Explore whether there are any accompanying thoughts with the emotion. (Some common examples would be: It's not fair. It doesn't make sense. I'm not good enough. I'm unlovable. I feel alone.)

Finally, imagine releasing the emotion. It has done its job: to alert you to a thought that needs addressing. It may not go easily, and it may come back, but for this moment, release the emotion to the Lord.

A printable version of this exercise is available online at: www.ditchthedrama.net.

Identifying Emotions and Their Source.

The next step is to identify the kind of emotion it is. Anger, fear, jealousy, shame, guilt, and then identify the person or situation to which it is attached. The name of the emotion is not always apparent. You may find it easier to identify the connection to the situation before the name of the emotion itself.

In either case, the next step is to identify the thinking that brought you to this emotion. Observe the thoughts you are having. Are they derogatory towards yourself? Are they hurtful towards someone else? Are they based in the truth of God or lies from the devil?

If they are lies, find the scripture that proves it. Find scripture that shines light on the lie. Memorize that verse or write it down and repeat it often. Because I am a visual learner, I will often put scripture on my bathroom mirror to remind me of His truth.

The best question to help you identify the cause is simply "why?" beginning with "Why do I feel this way?" and moving on to "Why do I think this way?" and then "why?" and then "why?" again until you find the root of the root cause. You should sound like a three-year-old. Actually, a lot of your thinking stems back from the belief system you adopted in early childhood. Your "why?" might just bring you back there.

For example, one of the things that caused me the most anxiety in life was fear that my boss would disapprove of my work performance. I had panic attacks over this and more than one weekend was ruined over worrying about his disapproval until I went through this "why?" exercise and kept backing up my logic.

The emotion was "fear" connected to my boss' approval.

"Why do you feel this way?"
Easy answer: His disapproval means I'll be fired.

"Why are you scared of being fired?"
I'd have to find another job. I could lose my apartment.

"Why are you scared of losing your apartment?"
I don't know. I wouldn't be homeless. I'd just move in with my parents. Ok, I'd have to find another job.

"Why are you scared of finding another job?"
I'm scared I won't find one.

"Why? What would happen?"
I'd move in with my parents.

"Why are you scared of moving in with your parents?"
I'm not. They're cool.

At the beginning of the exercise I gave myself what I thought were the right answers. The answer I thought I was scared of, but never actually bothered to ponder. I knew I had skills and could get another job. I knew the Lord would take care of me. I had to forget my rabbit trail and go back to the beginning.

"Why do you fear your boss' disapproval?"
Because I've always feared the disapproval of authority.

"Why have you 'always' feared this?"
When I was little I was scared to disappoint anyone.

"Why were you scared to disappoint anyone?"
Well, I was scared to disappoint my parents and I saw other authority figures in the same way.

"Why were you scared to disappoint your parents?"
I equated disappointment with a loss of love and worthiness.

"Why did you equate disappointment with a loss of love?"
I was punished when I did something wrong and my parents were disappointed.

That day, I discovered I was applying a childhood lesson with a grown up problem. The coping mechanism I used as a child to do my best to keep approval and love and avoid punishment, was no longer relevant as an adult. Once I recognized this, the power of that fear dissipated.

The next few times I felt that fear of disapproval I more readily recognized it. I reminded myself the origin of that fear was not appropriate. I asked the Lord to remind me that His love was more important and His love did not depend on my performance.

"But God, being rich in mercy, because of the great love with which he loved us, even when we were dead in our trespasses, made us alive together with Christ – by grace you are saved!"
Ephesians 2:4-5 (ESV)

Over time, it became easier and easier to shed the fear, until finally, I stopped being scared at all. Instead, I was more courageous in my work because I knew no matter what, I was loved by God.

It was easier to do my job after that. I was not distracted by fear and cyclical thinking of "what ifs." Because every time a "what if" started, I would end it with, "God will still love me."

By observing emotions, you become familiar with

thought patterns. By recognizing your thought patterns, you can fight their impact with God's truth.

If you start this process after years of emotional numbing and stuffing, over the first weeks and months you may feel as if the flood gates have opened and you experience a tidal wave of anger and other intense emotions. This is temporary and normal.

Have you ever held an inflated beach ball under water and then released it? The ball will shoot up into the air with extra force. It will land, eventually, and become still on the surface of the water. That is what can happen with emotions. They have been under pressure for so long, they come out at first with extra force. Have confidence that they will eventually rest in peace on the surface of the water once you stop stuffing.

In the mean time, this period of overflowing anger can be a confusing and scary time, particularly for anyone unskilled in expressing emotions or unfamiliar with feeling emotions.

> *"Let all bitterness, and wrath, and anger, and clamor, and slander, be put away from you, with all malice."*
>
> Ephesians 4:31 (ESV)

As your journey of serenity continues your goal is always to keep your emotions like that beach ball resting on the surface of the water.

Prayer

Heavenly Father,
Search my thoughts and remove any beliefs that are not rooted in
Your truth. Give me the strength to recognize my thoughts, and
feel my grief so that I may release toxic emotions and be healed for
Your glory.
I trust that You will complete this good work, which you started
in me. I know You will fulfill Your promise to comfort those who
mourn.
In Jesus' name, Amen.

5

THE THINGS I CANNOT CHANGE
What lies outside our control, really?

While there are many things in this world we would like to change (and we certainly try to change on a regular basis), there is only one thing over which we have control – and that is ourselves in this very moment. Not the moments to come or the moments behind us, but right now.

We have a choice in each moment about how to act or react. Everything else we must learn to accept.

And while much of what we need to accept is outside of our expectations, it does not follow that it must be a negative or hurtful reality we need to come to terms with. In reality, positive and healing truths can be just as difficult to accept if they do not fit into our expectations.

God's Love Is Uncomfortable.

The most important truth we can accept is the magnitude of God's love for us. This is a beautiful and wonderful truth, but that doesn't make it any easier to accept. We can wrestle with this idea because ultimately, we are not worthy. It may be more comfortable rejecting His love because we have more experience earning the love of others.

If the concept of grace and love is foreign to us, it will be that much harder to accept, especially for those of us who have not experienced grace or unconditional love from our nuclear family. But no matter the level of difficulty to embrace, the truth remains unchangeable.

The first lie ever told on the Earth was also the first words spoken by the serpent in the Bible. The identity of the serpent is known to us as the fallen angel Lucifer who wanted all of God's beauty and power. The lie he told is the most prolific and powerful lie told all the way from creation through today. This lie continues to be humanity's greatest downfall.

> *"Did God really say, 'You must not eat from any tree in the garden?'"*

Genesis 3:1

The true deception is found within the first three words. That's all it took. With just three little words the seed of doubt was planted: *"Did God really...?"*

After those three little words, any statement can be inserted to cast doubt on the person of God. The wide application is what makes this lie so dangerous.

The words are short and simple. Their purpose is to rip us away from our God of love and mercy and hope by pointing us toward despair and resentment. It is an attempt to destroy our relationship with God and thereby destroying our capacity to love for the purpose of harming God.

The serpent could not care one lick about humans except to use us as a tool to inflict pain upon God. His mission is to tarnish the glory of His kingdom for the purpose of gaining power. *"Did God really...?"* is meant to separate us from trusting the one God of the universe who desires to love us unconditionally, protect us from unnecessary harm, and forgive us completely.

But God will use this same hurtful question for good.

Because, on the other hand, for seekers of God, *"Did God really...?"* can be the start of a beautiful relationship with Him.

After all, seek and you shall find. Knock and the door will be opened. For determined seekers, *"Did God really...?"* is a loud knock at the door of God's kingdom. It is a glorious sound. It is the question asked by a heart who is eager for understanding and hoping to be loved.

It's understandable how we can be drawn to doubt, though. With so much pain in this world, we can become skeptical of God. *"Did God really...?"* is easier to accept than, *"Yes! God really!"*

I searched for peace in meditation, yoga, kickboxing, running, TV, relationships, work, wine, theatre, food, and cigarettes before looking to God. What stopped me was *"Did God really mean He would love you always?"* Because in the corporate, atheistic circles I had traveled amongst, faith was foolish. And looking foolish was a fate worse than death in those circles. One day, though, when I accepted *"Yes! God, really does love me always,"* my life changed direction.

Here's the truth of His promises:

- Yes! God really wants to protect you from harm.
- Yes! God really loves you unconditionally.
- Yes! God really wants to forgive your sins.
- Yes! God really sees your heart and loves you any way.
- Yes! God really has a plan for you in His love story.
- Yes! God really made you perfect.
- Yes! God really doesn't *need* your good deeds.
- Yes! God really doesn't base your importance on your performance.
- Yes! God really is making a place for you in heaven.

- Yes! God really loves you like His own child, a part of Himself.
- Yes! God really took your sin punishment so you could know love and mercy.
- Yes! God really can be trusted.
- Yes! God really has never left you or forsaken you.
- Yes! God really will never leave you or forsake you.
- Yes! God really is good.
- Yes! God really does use pain for good purposes.
- Yes! God really is omniscient, omnipresent, and omnipotent.
- Yes! God really hears your prayers.
- Yes! God really will give everything you desire as long as it is good for your whole journey.
- Yes! God really will never let you be tempted without an escape route.
- Yes! God really is for you!
- Yes! God really is working in all things for your good.
- Yes! God really can make you free if you follow His teaching.

Dwell on these promises. These are the most fundamental truths of our existence. You cannot change them.

Exercise: Affirming God's Promises

Take stock of your mood. How content do you feel on a scale of 1 to 5?

Say the promises above out loud. Spend a few seconds with each one.

Read through the promises again but this time put a check mark next to the promises you agree with and a question mark next to the ones you have difficulty with.

Monitor your contentment again on the same 1 to 5 scale. Do you feel any different?

Were there any promises that made you feel particularly safe or loved?

Which promises were difficult for you to accept and why?

A printable version of this exercise is available online at: www.ditchthedrama.net.

As much as you may be unfamiliar with this kind of love, mercy, forgiveness, and total acceptance regardless of your actions, these are truths you cannot change. Just as we cannot travel back in time and change the past, we cannot change the truth God has given to us. These promises are fixed. If we can accept these promises and make them part of our automatic thoughts and the foundation of our decision making (despite our fluctuating feelings), then drama and unnecessary pain drops to the wayside. Every good fruit you bear stems from these promises.

Stay vigilant in your belief of these truths. Immerse yourself in them day and night. Despite the many disappointments we will need to accept in life, God's truths are still the most important part of our reality.

Review these promises again – do you notice the theme of His power and our weakness? The Lord gives these promises to us because alone we are powerless in our brokenness. He promises to meet us where we are and He will make us enough in His power.

We are broken, yes, but we are not to despair in this truth. Broken does not make us evil or useless. Our part in this journey is to stop fighting and accept both our powerlessness and His powerfulness in our lives.

Exercise: What God Says About You

The Lord has also made it clear in His Word what you mean to Him and how much He cares for you. I have put together a list of verses and declarations He has made over His children. Repeat the exercise you completed with God's promises with this new list.

He has accepted you:

- I am a child of God (John 1:12)
- I am an heir of God since I am a child of God (Gal. 4:6,7)
- I am a friend of Jesus (John 15:15)
- I have been bought at a high price by the Lord (1 Cor. 6:19, 20)
- I have been established, anointed and sealed by God in Christ (2 Cor. 1:21, 22)
- I have been redeemed and forgiven (Col. 1:14)
- My debts have been canceled because the record of the charges against me has been nailed to the cross (Col. 2:14)
- My life is now hidden with Christ in God (Col. 3:3)
- I have been saved and set apart since before the beginning of time (2 Tim. 1:9)
- Jesus is not ashamed to call me brother (Heb. 2:11)
- I am a part of Christ's body (1 Cor. 12:27; Eph. 5:30)
- I am complete through my union with Christ (Col. 2:10)

He has sealed your place in His kingdom:

- I am a citizen of heaven, (Phil. 3:20; Eph. 2:6)

- I am seated with Jesus in the heavenly realm right now (Eph. 2:6)
- I have been given God's guarantee of my inheritance in heaven because I have received the gift of the Holy Spirit. (Eph. 1:13,14)
- I am free forever from condemnation (Rom. 8:1)
- I have been blessed with every spiritual blessing in the heavenly realm (Eph. 1:3)
- I may approach God with boldness and confidence (Eph. 3:12)
- I have been rescued from Satan's power and transferred to the kingdom of Christ (Col. 1:13)

He has made you significant:

- I am a saint (Eph. 1:1; 1 Cor. 1:2; Phil. 1:1; Col. 1:2)
- I am the salt of the earth (Matt. 5:13)
- I am the light of the world (Matt. 5:14)
- I am a branch of the true vine, able to bear much fruit in Christ (John 15:1,5)
- I have been appointed by Christ to bear lasting fruit (John 15:16)
- I was chosen before the creation of the world to be seen as holy and blameless (Eph. 1:4)
- I am Christ's ambassador (2 Cor. 5:20)
- I have the right to come boldly near the throne of God to receive mercy and grace when I am in need of it (Heb. 4:16)

Take stock of your mood. How content do you feel on a scale of 1 to 5? Say the truths below out loud. Spend a few seconds with each one.

Read through the declarations again but this time put a

check mark next to the declarations you agree with and a question mark next to the ones you have difficulty with. Monitor your contentment again on the same 1 to 5 scale. Do you feel any different? Were there any declarations that made you feel particularly safe or loved? Which were difficult for you to accept and why?

A printable version of this exercise is available online at: www.ditchthedrama.net.

Prayer

Heavenly Father,
Your love and generosity are staggering. Help me to accept the truths You declare over me. I believe in my heart that Your promises are true. I receive your unconditional love and care with an open heart.
In Jesus' name, Amen.

6

THE COURAGE
This one thing makes courage possible.

Courage is a trait that can only be discovered and proven in times of fear by venturing into new and uncharted territory. We can hope we would be brave in the face of fear but we never truly know the extent of our courage until we are put to the test.

Universally, we fear the unknown because of the increased possibility of feeling pain. And pain is relative. One person's level of fear for skydiving might match another person's fear of walking into a family reunion. Courage has less to do with the physical risks of the task and more to do with our perceived level of risk.

Real Courage.

If we live from the truth of God's promises outlined above, we are able to mitigate the fear. Leaning on God's power takes much of the responsibility off our shoulders. We are not alone. God is working for us. Let Him work for you.

> *"...If God is for us, who can be against us?"*
>
> Romans 8:31

Before I accepted the truth of God's promises, I felt the weight of every risk entirely upon my shoulders. Everything became something to worry about, prepare for, and brace for the worst, whether it was a meeting with my boss or first date, or plane ride.

But knowing His power and strength and presence are always with me, my courage has increased tenfold. I have faith in God's ability to protect me. I have faith that His will is better than mine. I have faith that the pain I feel and the challenges I face are there to strengthen me. I have faith that the fear I feel is a lie that is not from God, but from the brokenness of this world.

Courage is no longer about being responsible for the outcome. Courage is about showing up and surrendering enough to allow God to work for you.

At Jericho, the Israelite army had to surrender their ideas about warfare. They put down their swords and picked up their horns and walking shoes. The act of trusting the Lord with their success by passive walking may have been more difficult (and therefore more courageous!) than trusting Him to give them the city by the sword.

"Be still, and know that I am God!"

Psalm 46:10 (NLT)

This is God's command. "Be still," meaning to be surrendered to His instructions for them and stand firm in their faith. "Know that I am God," meaning, see for yourself that I am who I say I am and that my promises are true.

There is nothing in the definition of courage that says a man or woman must face their fears alone. We are stronger together, you and I, but we are unbreakable together with God.

Courage is not something we need to develop on our own. It is not a trait we need to conjure suddenly at our lowest point. It is something we can grow and cultivate with the support of God and others. Facing fear is a whole lot easier with back up.

So often we think, "This is my fear so I have to deal with it." But the Bible says:

> *"Cast your burden on the LORD and He will sustain you."*
>
> Psalm 55:22 (ESV)

We may think, "This is my fear, so no one else will understand it." But the Bible says:

> *"History merely repeats itself. It has all been done before. Nothing under the sun is truly new."*
>
> Ecclesiastes 1:9 (NLT)

We may think, "This is my fear, so no one else should be burdened with it." But the Bible says:

> *"Share each other's burdens, and in this way obey the law of Christ."*
>
> Galatians 6:2 (NLT)

There is no shame in asking for help. It's not cheating or creating false courage by relying on others. In fact, it takes great courage to be vulnerable enough to confess our fears and ask for help. Gaining support is actually the first step to facing fear. Our courage grows as we receive support, which eventually provides enough momentum to face the root fear.

When we are vulnerable and subsequently accepted by God and/or by others as we are, there is a great healing that takes place in us. There is a deep connection that is forged. That connection strengthens us and brings confidence we could never know on our own.

Prayer

Heavenly Father,
Increase my faith in Your power and promises so that I may face
every trial and challenge with the courage that comes from
trusting in You. Remind me that Your strength is available in
my time of need.
In Jesus' name, Amen.

7

TO CHANGE THE THINGS I CAN
What is within our control, really?

There are lots of things you might have influence over in your life, but there are precious few things you have complete control over.

I have said already that we only have control over actions in this moment. And there have even been times in my life – especially in the throes of addiction – when I felt I did not have control over my actions at all.

We have all been subject to knee-jerk, reflex reactions that we have regretted later. Maybe you told a secret you had promised to keep, or used hurtful words in a moment of anger, or allowed your inner critic free reign. We cannot control every aspect of our behavior at every moment. Congratulations, you are destined to screw up! Welcome to the human race. We are all broken and imperfect.

Part of being human is being subject to instinct and routine. Those two things lead us to inevitably do the same things over and over and think the same things over and over.

Our experience tells us that change and vulnerability are painful, so our instincts tell us to avoid change and vulnerability whenever possible. We are wired to protect the familiarity of routine, even a destructive routine. But changing the things we can means we must defy our instincts and routines.

For example, if you learned as a child that keeping quiet when a parent was angry would keep you from being spanked, you might take that "keeping quiet" routine into your adulthood and shut down at the first sign of conflict.

Every change starts with hope for a better future. We imagine our lives could look different – better. So we set a goal for ourselves. All too quickly we realize the change does not come easy or naturally. We must fight against our unconscious instincts and reflexes.

Remember, change is an exchange. We have to let go of our old behaviors in order embrace something new. You may have to grieve the loss of your old patterns before (or while) you take on new behaviors.

All of our emotions and actions are the by-product of our initial thoughts. These are thoughts about ourselves, the people around us, our values, and our beliefs. If we can change our thoughts – especially our knee-jerk automatic thoughts – we are in a good place to change our physical behaviors. And if you can align your thoughts to be in agreement with God's promises (outlined earlier), you will have a running start.

Changing Your Thoughts.

Think of your brain like a field. Your thoughts are like a car traveling over the field of your mind. Every time you have a specific thought, your car travels over the corresponding part of the field. The more often you have a thought, the more worn the field becomes.

At first it is just a path with tire marks, but as you continue repeating the same thought pattern, the small impressions turn into ruts. Your thought pattern will automatically want to drive in those ruts because they easier to drive in than over the unpaved wilderness around them. Eventually, when you think something even close to that rut, your brain car will move into the old, familiar ruts unless you intentionally steer your car away to build ruts in a different part of the field.

For example, perhaps one of the most common of the enemy's lies we believe is, "I'm not good enough." If you were to tell yourself repeatedly, "you are not good enough," it would eventually become an unconscious instinct to repeat the thought. Then, whenever you did not reach a goal or meet your expectations, your brain car would say, "Look! Here are the old, familiar ruts! *You're not good enough.*" It would not matter if you'd also achieved three goals or received a promotion that day. Your brain would see those ruts and go right for them! "You're not good enough, remember?"

It is possible to change these thoughts, however. There is definitely a way out. First, identify the negative ruts you want to change and then start building new ruts like "God made me specifically." Start repeating this phrase or any other of God's promises and start living like it's true.

Fight your unconscious instincts and reflexes with intentional effort. Keep your mind focused on the desired replacement thought while you make the effort to move towards the goal.

Changing your thoughts or habits is not a clear-cut fork in the road decision that Robert Frost would have us all believe. Taking the road less traveled by is a lot more complicated than a right turn. It's more like a zigzag back and forth from the new road to the old road until finally the new road veers so far off from the first road, we decide it is easier to stay with this new road.

As long as our eyes are on the prize and we don't give up, we can make the new road our home. At first, the effort will feel forced and uncomfortable. Keep repeating. As time goes on, that clunky, awkward thought will start to feel smooth and familiar. "I am good enough" or any other promise you repeat will ring out in your mind despite the messages from the world around you.

The devil's lies can most certainly be shattered, but God's promises are truth that cannot be broken. As long as you hold on to truth, you are standing on rock that will not move or weaken.

You'll make new ruts and make them deeper than your old ruts. Eventually, the wilderness of your mind will fill in your old ruts with debris and overgrowth as they become less and less familiar. Until one day you'll become so far removed from the lies they will feel like a hollow shadow of the past without power or substance, and wholly disconnected with present day.

This is a process - it almost never happens over night. How many times have you said this is the year you are going to regularly work out at the gym, only to have it last a few weeks? When you hit a challenge and you're forced to skip a day or two, you may or may not get back into the groove. It could help to enlist the company of a friend to keep you motivated, or you might change your morning routine to include a run instead. It's a process to discover what works best for you and how to keep your momentum going until it becomes a routine.

We may not be able to perform perfectly in every

moment or conflict. But, over time we can change the trajectory of our path.

Changing Perspective.

Perspective defines how we see the world. By taking a singular perspective, we may be fooled into seeing only one part of the story.

Consider a kaleidoscope. If you look through one end, you see beautiful colors multiplied in a multitude of angles. If you stopped there, you would think you held a beautiful piece of art. When you peer through the opposite side, you will see nothing. If that was the only view of the kaleidoscope, you'd think it very dull and useless. From the outside, it appears to be just a tube, perhaps a piece of pointless trash.

None of these perspectives is correct. You'd have to open the tube to see how all the perspectives work together. None of them are complete on their own. Together, they explain how the kaleidoscope works.

The same concept is true for conflict. No one person's perspective is correct, and if you can see beyond your personal perspective, you can see how the situation has truly come together as it has.

Since the 1960's doctors have been studying family dynamics. In 1968 Dr. Stephen Karpman developed a model of human interaction called the "Karpman Drama Model." It outlines three distinct roles in which individuals see themselves or see others in any given conflict: victim, rescuer, and aggressor.

The roles for each person are not fixed and can switch given the set of circumstances. This model has been generally accepted and I present these three roles to you now as perspectives you may take on a daily basis that may be creating or perpetuating drama in your life.

Victim Perspective.

As much as you may think life happens "to you" the reality is not that simple. It is easy to think "He/She did this to me" but from the other party's perspective they acted "for them." Most people do not intend harm to others, they are just too focused on meeting their own needs – consciously or unconsciously – to realize they may've hurt someone else.

We can even assume the role of being God's victim and think "God is doing this to me" (this could be a whole new rut of thinking in itself!). But the truth lies further outside this limited perspective.

Symptoms of victim thinking most often manifest as a need to avoid confrontation, such as blaming others and incessant complaining behind the backs of the offending party. It is easier for victims to stew in their version of reality rather than risk hurting others or facing their own responsibility in the conflict.

Because victim thinkers hold on to their resentments they are likely to exhibit passive aggressive behavior when they feel hurt. Slamming of doors, the silent treatment, sarcasm, biting or humiliating remarks in public are all examples of passive aggression.

Victims can get out of their poor perspective by voicing needs, communicating concerns early, and expressing their emotions on a regular basis.

In my teenage years I was particularly adept at victim thinking. My father and I had a strained relationship in these years, which I perpetuated. Instead of communicating my hurt feelings, I shut down. I gave him the silent treatment for a week.

In my mind, I was a victim of his insensitivity. The

atmosphere in our home was just plain awkward as I silently raged. And it was completely my fault. I was so busy blaming and enjoying what I thought was justified anger, I never stopped to communicate my feelings and needs and give him a chance to talk with me.

The best way to shed the victim perspective is to stand up and start fighting for yourself with your words. Communicate your needs, your wants, your concerns, your thought process and emotions. Over time, victim thinkers will see they can have an active role in their surroundings and relationships. They will speak up for what they need and prevent the opportunity to be a powerless victim.

Have grace with yourself and other victim thinkers throughout this process. And it will surely be a process. Start small. Start by making changes with trustworthy people first. Ask for their help in keeping you accountable in voicing your needs and emotions. Eventually this will become a familiar action.

Rescuer Perspective.

Serving and caring for others is definitely an honorable, Christian practice. But too much of a good thing, is still too much.

Remember the story of Mary and Martha when Jesus tells Martha to stop working (to save the world) to make dinner perfect, by comparing her to her sister Mary? He said Mary had chosen better by choosing to sit at the foot of the savior Jesus as a disciple. Yikes, Jesus! Way to hit all kinds of pain points for Martha!

Jesus is not saying preparation and service are discouraged. He did not say the work she chose was bad. No, He said Mary has chosen better. Basically, there comes a time when your sacrifice is hurting you more than it is

Ditch the Drama

helping others. Martha was missing out on the precious time she would have to spend with her good friend and savior, Jesus. That was simply better.

Those of us who take the perspective of rescuer or savior may not realize the negative effects. Savior thinkers put their needs last, leaving them exceptionally hungry for love and spiritual satisfaction. This leaves them weakened. Eventually, we will deplete our storehouses if we continuously give and do not take time to receive love and be fed by others' service.

In this weakened state, we begin to resent those who continuously take and take. Depression, exhaustion and outbursts of aggression are a common result. Like Martha's outburst at Mary "Help me! I can't do this alone! Jesus – tell her I'm right!" [paraphrased]

Jesus does not rebuke Martha with the intention of shaming her. He speaks plainly so she can learn to live more at peace.

We rescuers can help ourselves by making a few simple changes.

1. Rather than blindly serving out of compulsion and guilt, we can serve only when we desire to serve out of love. By checking our motivations, we discover where our boundaries truly lie. Plus, we will not build resentments when we serve out of out of our desire to be obedient and show love in His name.

2. Building more boundaries in our service. Although, theoretically, we believe we can do anything and everything, the reality is that we can't. Physically and emotionally we need to rest and recharge. We can prepare for this by saying "no" to volunteer

88

opportunities or even saying "no" to our own expectations. When I first purchased my house, I cleaned the floor whenever I had guests over. But over time, I realized my energy was wasted on the floor. When the guests finally arrived I had less energy to love on them in person. I have stopped worrying about the inconsequential dirt on my floor in favor of more actively loving my guests – and I believe Jesus would agree, that is the better choice.

3. Rescuers may feel the need to fix situations for others in the name of service and caretaking. This can be helpful at first, but eventually we must let others suffer the consequences of their actions. By avoiding those consequences Martha-types are robbing others of valuable life lessons.

Martha-types can feel this is a harsh and loveless act. I assure you, it does no one any good to take the brunt of the consequence upon yourself.

Have you thought about what Jesus might be teaching Mary in this situation? He says that Mary's choice to love on the savior is the better. But what happens when they walk in to dinner and Mary's responsibilities aren't completed? When Jesus' favorite dinner rolls are not to be found, will Mary not be embarrassed by her inability to attend to her responsibility for the savior? (I know it seems silly, but I happen to like dinner rolls.)

Mary could learn that in the day leading up to the savior's visit, she had been disobedient in her service the whole day leading up to her decision to sit at the feet of the savior.

If Martha insists on picking up Mary's slack,

Mary will never learn the importance of obedience and service for herself.

Aggressor Perspective.

Have you ever noticed that your need to be right can shut down your ability to love? That pesky ego nags to be fed and its voice can be so loud, we are distracted from our path to loving others.

The need to be right comes at a high cost. It often takes the form of resentment and holding grudges. We can begin to see more division in our relationships than empathy and connection. "Us vs. them" thinking creeps in.

Parents and kids. Teachers and students. Christians and atheists. Straight and LGBTQ. Black and white. Democrats and Republicans. I've seen divisive stances on each side. I am not accusing one group of being more divisive than the other. There is "rightness" thinking on both sides of the fence that prevents understanding.

Where have you stood personally? Have you believed you are right and labeled another group or another person as the enemy?

Or have you reached out to hear what is beyond the words the the heart of both sides of an argument? Have you stepped back from your pride and tried empathy to bridge the divide? Because the real enemy is hiding behind lies and manipulation. Connection is where healing begins.

Jesus cares less about whose opinion is right and more about the posture of our heart. Asking for forgiveness and actively loving on others takes us out of the aggressor role.

Loving our enemies helps us to see them as people and individuals who are just like us. Sure, they have different views, but their needs and fears are the same. Their upbringing and experiences have only lead them in a different direction.

Godly Perspective.

Victim, Aggressor, and Rescuer perspectives keep us trapped in our own small painful world. To escape these perspectives, I have offered some solutions. What they all have in common is the change toward a higher perspective – the greatest perspective – a Godly perspective.

Paul's letter to the Colossians says this:

> *"Think about the things of heaven, not the things of earth. For you died to this life, and your real life is hidden with Christ in God... So put to death the sinful, earthly things lurking within you... now is the time to get rid of anger, rage, malicious behavior, slander, and dirty language... Since God chose you to be the holy people he loves, you must clothe yourselves with tenderhearted mercy, kindness, humility, gentleness, and patience. Make allowance for each other's faults, and forgive anyone who offends you. Remember, the Lord forgave you, so you must forgive others. Above all, clothe yourselves with love, which binds us all together in perfect harmony. And let the peace that comes from Christ rule in your hearts. For as members of one body you are called to live in peace. And always be thankful."*
>
> Colossians 3: 2-3, 5, 8, 12-15 (NLT)

By aligning our thoughts with His, we come to see this world, and everyone in it, unified in one characteristic: we were all created by God. God's creation was cast perfectly from the overflow of His love and therefore something to be loved. All of it. Not just the pieces of our choosing. Not just the pieces similar to us.

We are called to love our enemies. But who are our enemies? Those who have done us harm (from our personal perspective) and those who wish harm upon us? By this definition every teenager is the enemy of their parents. And yet, there are a great number of parents who choose to love rather than hate their teens.

We have a choice. We choose our enemies by choosing hate, holding grudges and calling out for justice by claiming righteous anger.

How does the Lord handle His enemies? First, God chooses not to hate. He chooses to reach out in love to everyone. Whether we have turned our backs against Him, or slandered Him or hurt one of His children. He does not call out for justice – He pays our price instead. Over and over again He refuses to treat us as His enemies.

We are called to keep a Godly perspective and choose forgiveness over hate. We are to let our enemies choose their animosity rather than the other way around.

Changing Reactions To Responses.

We all have knee-jerk emotional reactions when we feel threatened or wronged. When I say threatened, I am referring to anything that challenges the status quo. This can be anything from insulting a person's intelligence to a threat of physical violence.

Do you know what your instinctual reactions tend to be? Do you evade the truth, hide from the threat, ignore the threat, attack the threat, try to control the threat? By instinctively reacting, we do not take the time to investigate the situation or our emotions.

Knee-jerk reactions come out of our instinctual need for

immediate preservation. Common reactions include: yelling, making threats, isolating, compulsive apologies, lying and manipulation. They rarely contribute to resolving a situation because reactions rarely address the root cause of the threat.

Imagine you have bad allergies, but instead of taking one pill daily for the allergy, you use cold lozenges for the sore throat, eye drops for itchy eyes, tea and honey for the postnasal drip and cold medicine to clear your sinuses. These treatments are like our instinctual reactions. You are left with numerous and ineffective treatments for one small problem.

Ultimately, we want to effectively respond to the root cause and neutralize the problem. This requires us to slow down, examine the situation and accept the things we cannot change first. If we refuse to accept that we are suffering from allergies, the symptoms will continue to wreak havoc.

Have you ever tried to explain your drama to someone disconnected from the situation? If it's often long and complicated (impossible to explain in two sentences or less), it's most likely a story of reactions. Each person is reacting to the other person's reaction. On and on it goes.

I had a good number of these long-winded stories. And although the back and forth drama hurt me, I also enjoyed telling the story. I enjoyed telling stories that vindicated me. I enjoyed receiving confirmation from my friends about my righteous victim status. I felt justified. I felt proud that I was not as crazy as the other person.

And there's the real problem – pride. On a certain level I enjoyed reacting and adding momentum to the drama because I used it to build myself up and put others down. Reacting was easier. I didn't have to see my responsibility in each conflict as long as I kept pointing a finger. I didn't have to forgive those who persecuted me as long as I held on to my right-ness.

Growing up in New Jersey, I encountered pockets of culture where drama is a way of life. Within them, you are expected to react and engage in conflict. For me, this kind of culture became toxic.

Remember my weekend down the shore with my girlfriends? We were bickering with each other and reacting to the hurt we were causing in the moment. We were not addressing the root causes of our sensitivity (grief and rejection). We instinctually reacted to the conflict we were creating in the moment. We actually found refuge in the drama because the deeper root cause was more difficult to feel and address.

Believe it or not, this behavior is not uncommon. The little pains provide a distraction from the much larger pain. As a result, we can choose (consciously or unconsciously) to continue reacting and bring momentum to the drama. Even though we may want to ditch it, drama has potential to become a comfortable place.

At a certain point, we may recognize the futility of fighting for a relationship based on a long line of reactions and we give up. Walking away or cutting off contact with the other person does not quash the drama. Now you have two people holding grudges, but they are moving in different directions. Those grudges are now two separate sets of drama.

The only way to avoid creating more drama is to respond and address the root cause. That may mean looking inside you, or that may mean sitting down with your "enemy" and talking about your feelings and motivations or asking forgiveness.

Does that sound horrible? Does the very idea make you

want to go screaming for the hills? I didn't say this would be easy. Certainly, God never said we would be called to walk an easy road. But He did say He would be with us every step of the way. He said our obedience would set us free (John 8:32).

Remember, in order to change, you must defy your instincts. You can only defy that which you are aware of. So, take a moment to identify your instincts. Think about moments when you felt threatened or wronged. Maybe it was when someone criticized you or hurt you. What was your first instinct? Did you want to lie or come up with an excuse to dodge the responsibility? Did you retreat and isolate? Did you attack them with your words to deflect your pain?

Exercise: Reaction Awareness

Write down five incidents in the past week or month that upset your serenity. For each event, describe the following:

1. Who/What incited the emotion?
2. Which of your needs was threatened?
3. Identify the emotion and the level of intensity on a scale 1-10 (frustrated, anxious, and guilty are not emotions – dig deeper!)
4. How your body felt.
5. What you wanted to do.
6. What you actually did.

Example:

1. Who/What: In a heated phone conversation with my husband when the call dropped. I assume he hung up on purpose.
2. What need was threatened: Feelings of love and belonging because you assumed they hung up on purpose.
3. Emotion/Intensity: Anger / 7
4. Body Felt: Shoulders were tense. Stomach in knots. Ears were hot.
5. Wanted to: Cut off contact for at least the rest of the day and ignore him.
6. What you did: Slowed down and remembered that isolation creates drama. Accepted that I cannot change his reaction. Accepted that this conversation needed to happen in person; texted him saying we'd

continue the conversation at home when we have both calmed down.

The best outcome will happen when you assess the situation and respond to what actually happened rather than react to your feelings of being threatened.

If you cannot think of five examples initially, keep the list handy and add to it as emotions come up. Take your time answering these questions. This exercise is a way for you to get to know yourself better. The more honest you are with yourself, the more equipped you will be to replace your reactions with responses.

Remember, your emotions cannot be wrong. This is not meant to shame you for poor behavior. The Lord is well acquainted with your emotions and reactions, it's time you were as well. He does not condemn you, so neither should you condemn yourself.

Once you've completed all five, reflect on your results. The pattern that emerges is important because it helps you identify where you are most vulnerable.

Are the inciting events similar? We can be threatened by a specific person because they are truly a physical threat. But other times we feel triggered because they remind us of a person from our past. It might not be the person who triggers our emotion, but what they threaten. Consider these areas of your life:

- *Feelings of value and worthiness*
- *Feelings of love and belonging*
- *Control of the situation/future*
- *Physical safety*
- *Family safety*
- *Job security*

- *Financial security*
- *Change of daily routine*

Do you react strongly from threats to any of these needs? Is there one or more that bring a strong physical fear reaction just thinking about it?

Most likely, these are the areas of your life in which you are not trusting God. Are you holding on to these details and attempting to handle them yourself? Are you hiding old wounds from others or even yourself? The fear we feel is in opposite proportion to our trust in God. The less we trust, the more we fear, and vice versa.

Trust the Lord to work all things out for your good. Worry will not secure blessings or prevent disaster. Worry will only steal happy moments from your days. Trust His will.

When these areas of your life are threatened, take notice of the thoughts and feelings inside you. These are the moments when it is crucial to slow down if you want to resist your instinctual reaction.

Steps 2-4 bring awareness to your emotional patterns. What set you off at an intensity level 8 and what set you off at a 3? What emotions did you feel over and over?

Step 5 brings awareness to your behavioral pattern as a result of your emotions. Is there a pattern in how you react to these events? Do you often follow your instincts and react? Or slow down and respond?

Bringing awareness to the pattern is half the battle. Knowing your vulnerability and how you tend to feel will help you identify the warning signs when you want to react in the future. This gives you a better chance of resisting the reaction and consciously responding in the moment.

If you do not see a pattern, continue adding examples. Use this as you move forward and write down your reactions on a daily basis.

A printable version of this exercise is available online at: www.ditchthedrama.net.

Once you are aware of your instincts, they are easier to resist. The next time that instinct rises, consciously decide to slow down. Recognize how you are feeling, and resist your knee-jerk reaction. You may even have to remove yourself from the room to prevent reacting. If you take a moment – or even days if you need them – to examine the situation, you can replace your reaction with a decision to *respond* in a way that addresses the root cause rather than your emotions. A *response* is designed to be appropriate in light of the action and not the surrounding emotional interpretations.

Even if you feel justified and comfortable making a knee-jerk reaction, we are called, as Christians, to resist the temptation. Instead, we are asked to stay humble and put down our pride and right-ness. We are called think of others' needs before our own.

We are not asked to ignore our own needs. Far from it. God has said, our needs are met through Him. Trusting His eternal love and care for our lives brings awareness that our needs are met. We are safe and loved and belong in His arms now and in the future. Trusting Him meets our needs and simultaneously makes us available to respond with humility to others.

The knee-jerk retaliation reaction is bound to get us sinning and creating dramatic waves.

Boundary Response.

If a dog were to bite you every time you tried to pet it, would you bring that dog into your bed every night? No, you'd probably put as much distance between you and the dog as possible. I know my hand, the only hand the Lord gave me, is way too precious to be putting it in harm's way all the time. I'd want to keep the threatening animal safely away from me in the backyard while I found it another home.

It sounds like common sense, right? But what if that biting dog is your family member, spouse or close friend? It still makes perfect sense to distance ourselves and create healthy boundaries from a dangerous threat. And yet, when we put a human face to the threat, it becomes harder to protect ourselves.

One noticeable trait that sets the human race apart from other animals is our desire to help one another. When we see someone in need, we come to their aid. Of course, this doesn't always happen perfectly, but as a race, we rally and help each other. It's a behavior we value and idolize. That's why our stories of heroes consistently glorify those who help other people at their own risk.

So, when we come to a place where our emotional or physical health is threatened by someone we value, we resist the urge protect ourselves in favor of sacrifice. After all, villains are selfish and turn their backs on the needs of others, right?

This is the kind of victim/savior/aggressor perspective we have to fight to ditch the drama. We are all God's children deserving love, respect, and healthy relationships. We are certainly called by God to love and help others, but not at the expense of repeatedly hurting ourselves.

I had always thought putting my needs before the expectations of others was selfish. Imagine my shock at realizing disappointing others would sometimes be necessary for my own emotional, spiritual, and physical health.

Just after graduating college, one of my best friends hosted a party to celebrate our newfound freedom from the seemingly endless tests and papers. The day came and I found myself sick as a dog with a cold. When I called her to break the news, I was told my presence was still needed because I was VIP in her life.

I was flooded with guilt. And because the last thing I ever wanted to do was disappoint her in any way, I decided to go. I peeled myself off the couch, packed some MucinexD, and drove over an hour to her home.

After our phone conversation I expected to be greeted at the door with joy and celebration. Instead, there was the usual "Hey, Ginny." From some familiar faces, and I was completely ignored by some folks I had never met before, all of them very drunk.

It turned out, my friend had celebrated too hard too early and she had passed out in her bed before I'd arrived. I was disappointed, to say the least. But, because I still had this idea I was VIP, I felt responsible for the party and spent the rest of the night cleaning up and protecting the house from spills and damage. My health had to wait another day to be attended to.

This was years before I recognized this was not what Jesus meant when He said "love your neighbor as yourself" (Matt. 22:39). I was putting my precious life in the mouths of violent dogs by trying to save them without regard to myself.

Around this same time, one of my boyfriends began to exhibit increasingly violent tendencies, first at bars and then inside his home, I began talking about the possibility of ending our relationship. His response was to start punching himself in the face.

The idea almost sounds comical, but I assure you it was terrifying to watch a kind of Fight Club type scene begin to unfold before my eyes. This was a man in training who spent more time at the gym than he did with me. He could have really done some damage.

My response was to assure him I would stay. Even though this was clearly another escalation of violence, I could not bring myself to cause him more pain. My instincts were to save others. I was completely unaware that I could be my own hero and save myself.

I let a parade of people lead me around. They bit down when they were unhappy. Some refused to let go. Others promised to be great companions and then bolted suddenly leaving me to tend my wounds alone. I was left lonely and hurting from my mission to avoid being selfish. The pain became so strong, I felt my only option was to crawl to the bottom of a bottle.

And then the day came when the Lord helped me to see myself through His eyes. He said, "Such a precious jewel needs to be cleaned and cared for, protected and on display. Why are you allowing these dogs to scratch and mistreat you?" Then He specifically pointed me to a scripture in Matthew I had previously misunderstood.

> *"Jesus replied: 'Love the Lord your God with all your heart and with all your soul and with all your mind.' This is the first and greatest commandment. And the second is like it: 'Love your neighbor as yourself.'"*
>
> Matthew 22:37-39

In this passage, Jesus says the most important thing we can do on this earth is love God, love others, and love ourselves. The verse does not say love others and forget about you. He calls us to have a balance by loving both others and ourselves equally (just behind our greater love of God).

I realized I was too wounded to help my companions or even help myself. That's when I ushered all of my friends to the "backyard" and closed the door between us. It was painful again to hear them crying for my attention and protesting my boundaries with more biting name-calling and accusations. But I knew that letting them close to me at that moment would only hurt both of us more. Eventually, they learned their cries were useless and they backed off.

I found myself alone and isolating from the world. I'd even kicked God out of the house for a time. But He never stopped knocking at the door. I found isolation was just as painful as being bitten. The fear of being hurt again prevented me from letting anyone too close for a time. God's knocking was subtle but persistent. He wasn't angry or threatening, more like gently reminding me of His interest.

One day, I trusted Him enough to let Him back in. The Lord, Jesus, and the Holy Spirit were with me. At first, we were a party of four nursing me back to health. Eventually, I called on my life-giving friends to come over and visit. Some stayed for a while to help. Others only came to drop off some life-giving nugget and walk back out. Although it was difficult to trust, especially at first, these visits were exactly what I needed to heal completely.

When I was healed and strong enough, I opened the door to the backyard where the "dogs" were waiting for me. I only stayed for a moment, and went back inside at the first sign of aggression. Over time, I was able to learn to use my words and body language to earn the respect of some of them. But, overall, they knew I would protect myself the moment they were aggressive.

Eventually, some of the previously threatening friends

became great companions and earned a spot in my inner circle. Others could exhibit nothing but aggression, which forced me to remove them from my life altogether.

You are precious too as the child of a King! No matter what has happened to you or what you've done, you are never too broken to receive love and healing. He offers them at every moment. All you need to do is accept.

Balance is the name of the game. On one hand, it's imperative to establish boundaries that keep you safe. On the other hand (pun not intended), be careful not to fortify boundaries so strongly that love cannot find its way in. With God's help, we discover how to be heroes in our own lives and in the lives of others.

There is a delicate balance. Be wary of whom you grant access to your trusted circle – your "home." Be wary of granting too few friends access as well. Expect a learning curve. There will be some pain along the journey as supportive people and vicious dogs come and go. But experience from the pain is a great teacher.

Discovering the right balance for your needs is something I will address in the chapters on Wisdom and Knowing the Difference.

Gratitude Response.

Practicing gratitude is like exploring the depths of the ocean. The more you explore, the more beauty and possibilities you discover. In time, you realize the depths of gratitude extend even beyond where humans can physically explore.

At its most potent, gratitude is a lifestyle. I'm talking a joyful, abundant, positive, peaceful, carefree lifestyle.

Let me explain. What do you think about when you are bored, or in line, or trying to fall asleep? If you're anything like the people I've coached or served as a speaker, I can be pretty sure you start rehashing all the things that need to get done and all the fears that come along with them. That quickly transitions into all the people and things that are in your way causing trouble. Am I right?

What if, instead of allowing that knee-jerk reaction, you actively focused on gratitude? Count your blessings one by one. Think on what you have rather than what you lack.

By recognizing the things we own, our job, safety, family, and friends as gifts from God, we recognize the true provider – and not just any old plain-Jane provider, but the eternal, ever-constant provider. Meditating on our gratitude to Him specifically strengthens our trust and connection to Him. The time we spend in that connected space is priceless because it naturally magnifies our joy and peace.

"Every good gift and every perfect gift is from above, coming down from the Father of lights with whom there is no variation or shadow due to change."

James 1:17

Just as we recognize abundance as a gift, we can recognize trials and disappointments as gifts as well. Every circumstance that we experience has been filtered through the hands of our Heavenly Father. Although no evil thing is from God, it may be His will that we be allowed to experience such pain. If you continue to trust Him, then you can be assured He will redeem that pain and use it for the glory of His kingdom.

"Consider it pure joy, my brothers and sisters, whenever you face trials of many kinds, because you know that the testing of your faith produces

perseverance. Let perseverance finish its work so that you may be mature and complete, not lacking anything."

James 1:2-4

If you cannot be grateful for grief, be grateful you can trust Him to bring you through. Be grateful He is walking with you through the pain. Be grateful He feels it with you. Be grateful the pain will be used to help another. Be grateful He can use you to give hope to others with similar pains.

There is always something to be grateful for.

We can thank Him for the sunrise, the beauty of His creation, and the carefully balanced nature in which we live. For He took great care to create the world and each inhabitant, including you. If you woke up this morning, then He is still writing you into His love story to the world. There is a role and a purpose that only you can fill.

I don't know about you, but that is an honor that humbles me daily.

Exercise: Mile High Gratitude

If you are impressed by quantity, then this exercise is for you. If you prefer quality and deep thinking over quantity, then move on the Gratitude Exercise Deep and Wide.

Every day write down 3-10 things you are grateful for. From the large to the mundane, you can be grateful for it all.

The only rule is that you cannot repeat anything on the list more than once.

Read through your growing list every day and watch your blessings pile higher and higher.

A printable version of this exercise is available online at: www.ditchthedrama.net.

Exercise: Gratitude Deep and Wide

Every day write down one thing you are grateful for. Below that, list all of the reasons you are grateful for that person, place, or thing.

For example, if I were to choose to be grateful for trees, I would make a list that looked like this:

Their shade, beauty, shelter for birds and animals, fruit, paper, wood-floors, timber for homes, fuel for fires, shelter from wind, their symbolism in the kingdom (roots grow stronger and deeper because of storms, seasonal changes, rebirth of leaves, their death provides for us).

A printable version of this exercise is available online at: www.ditchthedrama.net.

Forgiveness Response.

Forgiveness can be hard. I mean, really, really, really hard. And if you are holding on to resentments against a family member or someone you see regularly, it's even harder. There's a reason for that: forgiveness is counter-intuitive.

Our flesh, our rational side, and our justice system call for an-eye-for-an-eye type of fairness. There's no surprise there. We know that there must be consequences for wrong action because God deemed it so. It's woven into our worldly cultures because that is what God wove into our spirit and body. Our flesh actually cries out for wrongs to be righted.

"I will put my law in their minds and write it on their hearts. I will be their God, and they will be my people. No longer will they teach their neighbor, or say to one another, 'Know the Lord,' because they will all know me, from the least of them to the greatest."

Jeremiah 31:33-34

Are you familiar with the statue of Lady Justice? She stands outside so many courtrooms holding a scale. The concept is this: when a wrong has been committed, the scale tips one way, and it's the court's job to decide how to bring it back into balance.

When the balance of justice is off in our personal lives, we feel entitled to hold grudges and resentments. Our mind can swirl and keep coming back to the un-righted wrong over and over. Unless we consciously work to forgive, hours of anger can turn into days and into weeks and into years.

Somewhere in our subconscious we believe the only way we can ever possibly make things right again is by recognizing the wrong, keeping score until there is retribution somehow. In the meantime, all we can do is try to make sense of the hurt. We ask "How could you? How dare you?" or sometimes the question is simply "Why?"

I've been in this cycle of never ending questions. Rarely is there a satisfactory answer. Some things we will simply never be able to reconcile or understand from our personal perspective.

I said earlier that we automatically want justice for wrongs because God wrote that in our heart and spirit. That's how He set up His spiritual kingdom. Those are His rules. For the Israelites, He mandated the death of an animal for each sin they committed in order to keep them in right standing with God. Each wrong had a tangible consequence: a death.

The enemy would have us believe that is where the story ends. The serpent whispers that justice isn't justice until we can see, smell, taste, and feel retribution in this lifetime. He whispers until we can focus on nothing else and every cell of our bodies cries out for justice.

But our faith is in a God that is bigger than the physical world. He gives us faith in life eternal! When Jesus came on the scene, He encouraged radical forgiveness. Not just once or seven times but seventy times seven times. He didn't stop at preaching. He took action at the Lord's request. This Jesus, who was fully man and fully God, sacrificed Himself on the cross.

> "For God made Christ, who never sinned, to be the offering for our sin, so that we could be made right with God through Christ."
>
> 2 Corinthian 5:21 (NLT)

God created the rules. He also created this substitution

111

loophole whereby a sacrifice could be made in place of our own death. He took advantage of the loophole with Jesus. In that one act, He reconciled all manner of wrongs and sins for as long as this physical world goes on. He paid the price. He paid the consequence.

When we cry out for justice, we have to remember Jesus has already endured the consequences. Justice has already been paid. Revenge has already been served. And not just for our perpetrators, but for us as well.

Remember Lady Justice with her scale? Jesus made sure the scales were always balanced. No matter how many sins are placed on our side of the scale, Jesus' actions are enough. The scale will not tip.

What makes this fair is that forgiveness is offered completely to everyone. There is no measure of how wrong or right any one of us can be. Because we have all sinned and all caused hurt, we are all offered the gift of forgiveness.

"But I tell you who hear Me: Love your enemies,
do good to those who hate you, bless those who curse
you, pray for those who mistreat you."

Luke 6:27-28

Exercise: Finding Forgiveness

The following are a series of exercises you can walk through to help you release anger and resentments.

1. Pray for your enemies:
   - *For their salvation*
   - *For the softening of their hearts*
   - *For conviction of their sins*
   - *For their closer relationship with the Lord*
   - *For their ability to love and forgive others*
   - *For blessings in their life*
   - *For their healing*

2. Love your enemies. Here are some ways to show love:
   - *Give them gifts*
   - *Pay them authentic compliments*
   - *Listen to them without judgment*
   - *Reassure them with a friendly touch*
   - *Volunteer to help them*

3. Make a list of all the good your enemy has done for you and the world. No act is too small (no person is all bad).

4. Write a letter you never intend to send. Express how they've hurt you and express why you've decided to forgive them and leave justice to the Lord.

5. Tell the story of the wrongdoing from your enemy's point of view.

6. Tell the story of the wrongdoing from God's point of view.

7. Ask yourself, "What part was my responsibility in all this?"

A printable version of this exercise is available online at:
www.ditchthedrama.net.

Because He loves you so completely, belief is all you need to avoid suffering the consequences of those sins throughout all of eternity. Yes, in your short years here on earth, there will be physical consequences for sin, but for *eternity* you are forgiven.

This is not a get out of jail free card. We must exercise repentance and seek to love Him more. Those who do not believe may still suffer consequences in eternity. That is for the Lord to judge. He is the only one who can see our hearts without bias. Either way, we can trust His justice will come in the right time of His choosing.

Releasing Resentments.

Now, remember that anger and resentment are two different things. Anger is a healthy and necessary part of the grief cycle. Resentments are the dangerous cancer that is created when the cycle gets stuck on anger. Don't be too hard on yourself if you have resentments. You are part of a very large club called the human race. In this club we understand resentments are easy to make and keep.

At first, they seem comforting and justified, almost like an old friend. But after a while, the resentment becomes a burden.

In the mid 2000's I was plagued by panic attacks due to years of burying my resentments. I was trapped in an emotional cycle characteristic of codependents. First, I approached relationships very passively. But by denying my own needs and feelings I created (almost) subconscious resentments that eventually spilled out into passive aggressive behavior. Once the pressure had reached a boiling point, I would have angry outbursts followed by deep shame. I'd get back on the hamster wheel and try again to mend the relationship by being passive.

It was during this time I was suddenly forced to deal

with an incident from my past. My freshman year, I experienced an attack on my college campus. The incident and the emotions were startlingly painful. When I reached out to my friends for understanding, I was met with suspicion and questions. I deduced my pain was somehow wrong. After a week or two I stuffed my emotions down and pretended they weren't there.

Eight years later the effects of that incident were wreaking havoc in my life. I was acting out against people I loved. I decided it was time to get help from a professional and at the same time withdraw a bit from my extroverted social scene. I needed to cocoon and really take care of myself for the first time.

I wish I could tell you my resentment was held against my attacker. That would seem appropriate, right? Actually, that was the first person I forgave. And I did it easily. The hardest part was dealing with the backlash of a close friend.

Our friendship was extremely close. Too close to be healthy, really. My role was to make sure she was taken care of. I liked this role because it made me feel needed and important. Consciously, I didn't much care that I was completely passive. Unconsciously, I was ignoring my own feelings to fulfill the role.

She had a hard time understanding that I was deeply affected by the attack, and that I needed time away from her. She reacted with inappropriate and very public aggressive and passive-aggressive attacks. From where I stood, I was being punished for meeting my own needs instead of meeting hers.

Months later we had the opportunity to talk privately. She expressed her hurt. I apologized for my part because I never consciously intended to hurt her. And although I restated (twice) she also hurt me very deeply, she did not apologize.

This was too much for me to just overlook. How could I even think of forgiveness when a simple "I'm sorry" was not uttered? This is a basic, polite rule of society along with please, thank you, wipe your feet, don't spit on the birthday cake and, if you do, at the very least say "I'm sorry."

It felt like the wound reopened but now there was rampant infection. I was sure I was entitled to an apology. After all, I was the one who was publicly cursed out and embarrassed. I had to be right about that. And that's exactly what I clung to: being right. Those familiar questions of *How could you?* and *How dare you?* and *Why?* only circled faster.

The road to forgiveness was a long, eight-year stretch. I spent hours journaling, thinking, praying and empathizing. For long stretches of time, I believed I was successful, but then I'd run into a trigger and my resentment would pop up again. And I'd forgive again. Over and over.

The most important thing to understand about resentments is that all of them require we believe the lies of the enemy. You might remember from the first two chapters I described how the serpent deceives by encouraging our doubt in God. If we believe God is holding out on us, then we can be persuaded to act on our own selfish desires, including holding onto resentment.

Here are just a few of the lies the enemy wants to trap you with:

Lie #1: Resentment gives you control.

When we are hurt, we naturally recoil to protect ourselves, and that's needed. But resentment builds when we stay there and refuse to work through the feelings. We succumb to the illusion that by holding on, we don't have to feel hurt. Similarly, we believe this resentment will protect us from getting hurt again as long as we have it.

While we nurse our wounds and rest in what we think is a controlled environment, we overlook that we have backed ourselves into a corner. Instead of allowing ourselves to walk through the grief process and heal in a healthy way, we cover over the heart wound with whatever dirty rags we have lying around so we don't have to look at it. We know it's there, infected and hurting under the surface, but our fear of being unable to control the bleeding has us throwing more and more junk on top of the infected wound.

Really, the only thing you are controlling is your limited ability to give and receive love. An emotional wound of the heart behaves very much like a physical wound. As long as you let the resentment fester, the heart's ability to receive and give love to others will be diminished.

Closing yourself off in an attempt to control your heart certainly has the illusion of safety. But isolation is another deadly tool of the enemy. Being vulnerable is part of how God allows us to thrive. It is a gift.

Think about it. Without vulnerability, we would not be able to build relationships. Without relationships we are drawing on our own singular abilities to process events and emotions, to feel loved, uplifted, and valued. It won't take long before we implode.

Forgiveness is not what makes you vulnerable. You were already vulnerable. Forgiveness opens your heart to receive healing from the Lord. Resentments open your heart to the enemy.

Lie #2: Guilt is only as good as the resentment.

You may have noticed that it's difficult to be content

with keeping resentments inside. Often, we want to shout them from the rooftops and tell everyone we meet. Eventually, we might bite our tongue out of guilt or obedience to the Lord. But there's usually a desire to complain and share how we've been mistreated.

Complaining about injustice is our way of seeking validation for our pain. We want to make sure people know we feel like a victim. This helps in two ways. First, the more people we find to agree with our victimhood, the more justified we feel in our resentment (read sin). Second, we feel the guilt of the other party is somehow more real and tangible if others agree.

It is a misconception to believe your resentment is the only thing declaring your perpetrator guilty. This is just another strategic seed of doubt planted by the enemy.

Forgiveness is not the same as declaring a person innocent. God is the only one who can rightly declare guilt or innocence. He does not waive someone's guilt because you have offered forgiveness.

God is the only one with authority to judge guilt or innocence. He is the only impartial being who sees the truth of all things in the universe. By personally assigning guilt and demanding justice you are declaring your knowledge and righteousness is above the Lord's.

Job was a man described in the Old Testament who's suffering, grief and confusion brought him to challenge God and His justice. I enjoy God's response because it's sarcastic! He shows some personality! Here's what He said:

> *"Will you discredit my justice and condemn me just to prove you are right? Are you as strong as God? Can you thunder with a voice like his? All right, put on your glory and splendor, your honor*

and majesty. Give vent to your anger. Let it overflow against the proud. Humiliate the proud with a glance; walk on the wicked where they stand."

Job 40:8-12 (NLT)

The wonderful thing about this passage is that God does not condemn Job for crying out to God in frustration and pain. He does not condemn Job for questioning the sovereignty or perfect justice of the Lord. He simply rebukes Job for believing he could possibly have all the answers. In Job chapter 38 He corrects Job by showing how his limited perspective could never account for the mysteries of how the universe works or how Job's justice would play out in the future.

In the same way, we have a limited perspective of the universe and others. We cannot make accurate judgments. It is for God to decide guilt. It is for us to surrender our desire to control who is declared guilty.

Again, we return to surrender and acceptance. He is trustworthy in all things, including judgment. He can be trusted to judge and give consequences rightly in His timing.

Lie #3: Your resentment hurts someone else.

No one suffers from your resentments more than yourself. You are the one who continues to feel the pain. You are the one who keeps the wound open. You are the one who chooses to let it fester and hurt you over and over.

By declaring guilt on another person, you also declare yourself a victim. But you do not have to be a victim any longer. You can choose to be an ex-victim by choosing forgiveness. It is not a gift to your enemy; it is a gift to yourself.

Have you heard the idea that holding resentments is like

drinking poison and expecting the other person to suffer? It's true.

One of my friends in recovery puts it like this: Resentments are just about as productive as peeing in your pants. Forgiveness is getting a clean pair of pants and moving on.

Lie #4: You've done nothing wrong.

Even though it poisoned my attitude and disrupted my joy and peace, there was always something nice about that familiar feeling of being right. Until one day it disappeared. I was listening to a lesson on forgiveness, which normally would have immediately brought the resentment to the surface. On this day my old friend "right" wasn't there anymore. "Right" had been replaced by sadness.

You see, I had finally worked it through. I had been stuck on anger because I so badly did not want to look at my own part with my unapologetic friend. Resenting was easier. It was safer than admitting my part. It was easier to believe it was my job to keep score rather than trusting the Lord's approach to justice.

The truth was, I was disappointed in myself. I could have made better choices and established a much healthier friendship. I could have expressed what I wanted and needed much, much earlier. I could have set more boundaries. I could have refused to sacrifice my time and money and self-respect for the approval of others.

Instead, I chose to disrespect myself. Knowing, all these years later, how precious a creation I am to the Lord, I felt I had let Him down by willingly putting myself in harm's way. I had cast my pearls in the mud to be trampled.

I asked forgiveness from the Lord and asked forgiveness of myself. Freedom arrived once I was able to accept both.

Prayer

Heavenly Father,
You made all the pieces of the universe and the laws of justice. I
confess that I have relied on the popular ideas of this world as my
guide rather than Your Word.
I ask Your forgiveness and I ask for Your help in fighting my
instincts from the flesh. Show me the thoughts and reactions,
which do not please You, so that I may align them with Your will.
Give me the strength and courage to follow You.
In Jesus' name, Amen.

8

WISDOM
The Two Most Important Questions

A suburban town once held a scavenger hunt for residents with a prize of $10,000. Two contestants, Ken and Susan, gained a big lead ahead of the others early on. They were neck and neck for most of the hunt until they received the last clue - finding a statue of a war hero on the south side of town.

Both contestants were unfamiliar with this particular part of town and neither were sure where to start. Ken scoured the area, looking in every park and at every school and town building until he finally found the statue. To his surprise, Susan had arrived first and claimed the prize money.

"How did you get here so quickly?" he asked. "You said you didn't know where to find it."

"Oh, it was easy," Susan replied. "I stopped and asked for directions."

The moral of the story is this: the beginning of wisdom is in knowing we don't have all the answers.

The Miriam Webster dictionary defines wisdom as the knowledge that is gained by having many experiences in life. By this definition, our omnipresent God has experienced all time and is, therefore, the keeper of all wisdom.

Human lives are limited. From a practical perspective, we cannot live as long as God has lived and therefore, individually we cannot have anywhere near the same amount of experiences as the Lord.

Still, there are a number of resources available to us where we can gain wisdom.

History.

Surely we have wisdom if we can learn from the great writers and historians that have existed over thousands of years, right? Yes, you could definitely read histories and biographies and autobiographies day and night and have greater perspective.

The Bible.

The Bible includes a number of histories and practical writings. It includes the history of God, and includes the many motivations of God throughout His history before, during, and after the human race. The words are inspired by God and their application to our lives is revealed by the Holy Spirit inside each Christian.

Human Nature.

Studying psychology and discovering the many tendencies that occur naturally within the human condition can uncover many secrets of interpersonal relationships. When we understand our motivations all come from the same place, we can begin to feel more connected with others and forgiving of their hurtful behavior.

Osmosis.

There is no greater learning experience than forced immersion. For example, when a foreign language student reaches a certain level of understanding, the teacher will begin to speak entirely in the new language so that student has even greater exposure and experience with the language. As a student of wisdom, there is no better learning experience than surrounding yourself with wise individuals. You'll begin to learn from their example and request their counsel on a regular basis. Eventually, the immersion in wisdom will in effect "rub off" on you.

Three-Dimensional Wisdom.

But even if you were to do all of these things, your wisdom would still be two-dimensional. That is, it would be limited to the knowledge of the past and present. God is the only one who has experienced three-dimensional wisdom by having experienced the past the present and the future. Not only that but He is omnipotent. He has had my experiences and your experiences and your children's experiences. He is not limited by space and time, therefore, He is the keeper of wisdom.

And yet wisdom is much more than knowledge and experiences. It is more valuable than mere facts and much more elusive. It is, in fact, the art of applying knowledge to life's present circumstances in order to understand God's will.

Applying The Serenity Prayer.

In theory, applying the Serenity Prayer to our circumstances should be simple. All we have to do is 1) examine the people and things in any given situation, 2) label what we can and cannot change, and 3) move forward to change the things we can. Unfortunately, theory is not reality.

In reality, life is rarely simple. We have very real beliefs and attachments, which complicate our perspective. Emotions impede our rational thinking, muddy the water, and life gets messy. When we stop trusting the Lord and follow our fear far enough down the rabbit hole, the light of hope can feel very small and far away.

When it feels as if you cannot put one more ounce of energy into crawling out of the hole, you have come to the end of all you can do for yourself. These moments are proverbial forks in your life's road. How you choose to deal with these moments will determine your path.

Choosing despair leads to destructive coping mechanisms. Food, TV, alcohol, shopping, isolating, can all be destructive when they are used to numb our emotions and distract thoughts.

On the other path, we can choose to surrender our striving and let God take over. We can trust that when we give up trying, we will not loose, but rather we will gain from His involvement in our struggle. We can trust that He will either change the things we cannot, or He will change our heart to accept them.

"The Lord will fight for you; you need only to be still."

Exodus 14:14

While these dark, definitive moments are bound to happen, they do not have to engulf us. By using the Serenity Prayer regularly, we develop skills to examine our emotions and see situations clearly. We can respond appropriately to the situation rather than thoughtlessly reacting to our initial fears or staying frozen in our fears. That response can nip drama in the bud and prevent spiraling into hopeless moments of despair.

To avoid drama, the two questions we must ask

ourselves in any situation are these:

1. What am I powerless to change in this situation?
2. What can I change in this situation?

If you can answer these questions keeping in mind the principles we've already discussed, then half the battle is already won! Our answers will clearly define where we can best put our energies moving forward. We can get off the hamster wheel and move forward. No more countless hours will be spent on fruitless endeavors. We can reclaim those valuable hours working toward attainable goals.

To give you an idea of how these questions can be answered in real-world situations, I've provided a few examples.

Example #1:

Your mentor asks you to lead a Bible Study. It is a 12-week commitment. You want to help her out and you want to be a servant to the Lord, but you know this kind of commitment will drain you significantly.

What are you powerless to change?

- God's love: He will love you whether or not you lead the class.
- God's will: If it is His will to pour life into these students, He can work it out with or without you.
- Your mentor's reaction: You cannot change how your mentor will feel if you turn her down.
- The finite amount of time you have available: You will be stretched thin on time and energy by teaching the class, which will put a strain on your body and your relationships.

What can you change?

- Seek wisdom by praying and asking God to help you discern His will.
- Enforce your boundaries by declining the opportunity, and choose to focus on your family.
- Shift your energy by accepting the opportunity and sacrificing another responsibility.
- Ask your family for their input before you decide.
- Ask your mentor to keep asking other people while you consider the position.
- Choose to lie awake at night worrying what the "right" decision will be.
- Choose to trust that God will work all things for your good and the good of your mentor and the students.

In these situations, there is no "right" or "wrong" decision laid out in the Bible. We must reflect on our own experience and our own walk with the Lord to determine where He is calling us. We must weigh the likely consequences of our decisions and trust that He will guide us and work it out no matter what.

Example #2:

Your 9-year-old daughter gave a compliment on the bus to her friend, Kera. Kera misunderstood what was said because now Kera's mother is sending you angry text messages and calling your parenting "careless."

What are you powerless to change?

- The past: The words were said and feelings have been hurt.
- Other people's emotions: The misunderstanding has clearly touched a nerve in both Kera and her mother.

- God's instructions: Love your enemies. Forgive your enemies. Live at peace with everyone as far as it depends on you.

What can you change?
- You can react and send a biting reply - *or*
- You can slow down before you react out of hurt.
- You can ask your daughter what happened before you respond.
- You can forgive Kera and her mother for their strong reaction before you reach out and respond.
- You can give Kera and her mother the benefit of the doubt that they are reacting out of old hurts.
- You can pray and ask God to help you in resolving the situation.

In moments when we are unjustly accused, the Bible is clear on what we are to do: love and forgive. It may feel difficult and unfair to be the bigger person. But God's instructions are not rules for the sake of rules. They are a blueprint to help us live fully by maintaining healthy relationships, resting in Him, and contributing to His love.

Example #3:

Suppose you have a good relationship with your mother and sister. However, they are not on good terms with each other. Instead of working it out on their own, both your sister and mother call you to vent their frustrations.

What are you powerless to control?
- Other people's emotions: You cannot make anyone else forgive.
- Other people's actions: You cannot make anyone respond effectively instead of reacting destructively.

- Our responsibilities: Accept that you are not responsible for your mother's and sister's relationship. It is their issue to work out. Not yours.
- God's love: You cannot change that God loves both of them equally, even if you want to side with one of them.

What can you change?

- Your perspective: You can choose not to label either person as "wrong" and see both of them as hurting and confused children of God.
- Your reaction: You can stop trying to change their perspective and emotions.
- Your boundaries: You can refuse to speak to either of them about the argument because it only creates drama to be in the middle.
- Your response: You can choose to pray for their relationship and request God's wisdom in setting your boundaries.

When drama is pushing into our life from more than one side we can feel powerless to change anything. The truth is, we can usually create some boundaries to keep us safe and separate from the storm. It can seem heartless at first. But this is not a decision made from a place of uncaring or unfeeling.

Boundaries do not separate us from our love. They separate us from the harmful consequences of others' decision to react and create drama. Separating yourself from others' conflicts is often an act of self-preservation. You can still care about the harmful consequences of others' decision while protecting yourself from the harmful outcome.

Exercise: Daily Serenity Worksheet

Answer these simple questions:
What am I grateful for today?
What wisdom have I learned today?
What am I trying to control that I need to surrender?
What do I have control over that I can actually change?

By answering these questions on a regular basis, you are reinforcing the wisdom and gratitude you feel in addition to bringing clarity to your circumstances. The more you practice, the easier it will be to apply the serenity prayer principles and neutralize your drama.

A printable version of this exercise is available online at:
www.ditchthedrama.net.

A deep understanding of the things you can and cannot change comes through observation and experience. Even a wise person is not free from making mistakes or making foolish decisions. A wise person will make foolish decisions and learn from them after reflection. A foolish person will repeatedly make the same foolish decisions based on the same false assumptions.

Which one are you? Maybe a little of both? I certainly have made both foolish and wise decisions in the past. But studying the serenity prayer will give you a greater understanding of the application of wisdom.

Prayer

Heavenly Father,
It is Your wisdom that is true. Help me to learn from the examples
in Your word. Give me insight into which aspects of my life need
accepting and which need changing. I trust Your Holy Spirit to
guide me and provide revelation.
In Jesus' name, Amen.

9

TO KNOW THE DIFFERENCE
Putting Wisdom Into Practice Every Day

Adam and Eve ate from the tree of the "knowledge of good and evil" and received knowledge. Unfortunately, they did not eat from the tree of "wisdom between good and evil." Wisdom is not a natural gift for most people. It comes from a series of learning experiences.

But there are practices you can use to apply wisdom beyond your years. I'd like to introduce you to my approach to wisdom. It comes from many painful experiences learning the hard way and some very wise Biblical verses. They will help you discern between the things you can and cannot change as well as clarify where God's will is leading you to act (if at all).

There are ten Wisdom Practices. You can apply these to any situation that will help you to discern the will of God. These are especially helpful when emotional circumstances have hijacked your ability to think clearly. Depending on your level of turmoil, you may need to use anywhere from all ten to two or three practices. Try each strategy or exercise until you are comfortable navigating the situation.

The more you do this, the more intuitive it becomes and the easier it is to apply each practice. Take your time with any step you do not fully understand, especially when you are first learning them. It will not benefit you to gloss over any parts you may not understand. It may feel awkward now, but, over time, you will find yourself using many of these practices automatically.

One - Slow Down.

The first part of receiving wisdom is seeking God's plan. Decisions made in the height of emotional situations are often reactive. The problem with reactive decisions is they are one-dimensional, consumed completely by the emotions of the present and failing to recognize the importance of the past and the future in the decision.

Take a deep breath and try not to make any decision right away unless absolutely necessary.

Two – Pray.

You never have to go through any difficult situation alone and powerless. God is with you. His power and wisdom can be called on to help you at any moment.

It is not weakness to ask for help, it is bravery to admit weaknesses and vulnerability. And you were not made to face life alone. You were made to walk this life with the Lord's help. You wouldn't cut off your right arm just before you entered a fistfight. Do not ignore the power the Lord has in your life before you enter a difficult battle.

Three – Release Emotion.

It is extremely difficult, almost impossible, to think with a clear head with all your emotions getting in the way. Remember, the first part of the serenity prayer is to ask for, you guessed it, *serenity*. The exact opposite of high emotions.

Sometimes all it takes is a few deep breaths, counting to ten, or distracting ourselves with gratitude for a moment.

Other times, this process can take weeks.

Remember that you are the true victim of your resentments. Go to the gym and work out your aggression, write a note, symbolically leave it at the foot of the cross (use a God box to put your worries in or tear up and throw out a list of the enemy's lies and stressors).

Four – Explore the Situation from an Outside Perspective.

First, see your part from a third-party perspective as objectively as possible. This should be easier after releasing many of your high emotions.

Remember that motivations are complex. No one is completely correct or completely hurtful in any interaction. Allow yourself to see where your weaknesses are and where your mistakes have taken place.

I like to take God's perspective first. I remember that both myself and my attacker/aggressor are loved by God no matter what mistakes we've made. I see my actions and feelings as being influenced by my past hurts and insecurities as I move around below God's feet. I see my attacker, whose actions and emotions are a result of their own past hurts and insecurities.

I imagine God must be hurting that we are at odds. His two children - whom He loves dearly - are in pain, and His heart hurts to see it.

Taking those emotions to heart, I next try to see the conflict through the eyes of the other person (no longer labeled attacker in my heart). I try to imagine what kind of fears and anger and hurts must they be feeling to have been motivated to behave in the way that hurt me.

We nearly always see the world as happening to us, at least, that is often our first, instinctual reaction. Conflict between two people really means there are two or more people who each see themselves as the victim. And what they are really crying out for is recognition of their hurt and acknowledgement that their feelings and opinions are significant.

Many times this exercise takes me out of feeling like the only victim in the situation. It allows me to recognize the second victim and how they are hurting. And as a result, I often find the hurtful part I played in the situation. It is embarrassing, but I am sustained by the knowledge that I am not a bad person for my actions. My God still loves me and I am still His priceless child despite my failings.

Five – Break Down The Moving Parts Objectively.

Define what happened in the most general terms possible. That means no name-calling, angry adjectives or assumptions or opinions. Stick to the facts. Simply state what happened.

This will help you gain clearer perspective of what transpired. It takes you out of your struggle to assign proper guilt to one party. (And, if nothing else, it is necessary to perform the next step properly.)

Think of it as a police report for an accident.

For example: Person 1 was traveling down the road of life at 35 miles per hour heading toward heaven. Person 2 was traveling parallel with Person 1. Person 2 hit an ice-cold memory of the past and the vehicle began to fishtail. Person 1 recognized what was happening and in an attempt to help Person 2 regain control of the situation drove closer to person 2. Person 2 saw Person 1 get closer and fearing they would hurt Person 1, slammed on the brakes and overcorrected the wheel, which sent Person 2 crashing into Person 1.

Both vehicles were sent skidding off the road on the

heaven bound side and came to a stop in a ditch just off the shoulder. After three days of shock and processing emotions in their own vehicles, Person 2 finally got out of their vehicle and approached person 1 to make amends.

Person 1 did not attempt to speak to Person 2 and drove away. Heaven bound with a damaged vehicle.

Sometimes there is no guilt or blame to be had. And we are left only with the consequences of two flawed people navigating dangerous situations.

Six – Compare and Contrast.

God is the master of metaphor. Long before Jesus was teaching parables, God used prophets and the weather and the elements to symbolize His kingdom, His love and His anger. In fact, all of creation is a metaphor pointing to the workings of God's kingdom.

The workings of God's kingdom are as complex as they are vast and timeless. It would be impossible for God to answer our questions directly. We are simply too limited in our understanding of the universe. It is no more possible for my cat to understand the workings of calculus than it is for us to understand the workings of His kingdom. It's not that we are stupid or that He is being secretive. It's simply not within our capacity to understand eternity with our human brain.

Instead, the Lord has used metaphor. This allows Him to compare some lofty, unrecognizable concepts to practices and routines we use on a regular basis. He has used families, farming, prostitution, marriage, pay days, jail time, debt, food, alcohol, taxes and many more common practices to explain spiritual concepts to millions of people spanning over thousands of years and lifetimes.

Each metaphor proves to be a masterful stroke of

genius. Because within each metaphor is several layers:

1) There is the literal story within the metaphor.
2) There is the comparison of worldly behavior to the spiritual kingdom.
3) There is the moral of the story showing us how God wants us to live our lives as Christians.
4) There is the deeply personal and practical application to your current circumstances.

In 2014, just around Easter time, I was studying the book of John. I came across the story of the woman at the well. (John 4:1-40) I read the literal story at first. And then I felt prompted by the spirit to look deeper at the message. So I read it again, but this time I looked for the metaphors. This passage has no shortage of metaphors, but there were a few that resonated with me that I will share with you.

First, I took the "just the facts, ma'am" approach. And the first thing I notice is that Jesus is talking to a woman who is considered a half-breed Israelite by the Jewish population Jesus was born into. He reveals Himself to her as the messiah by showing her He is intimately acquainted with her life's jacked-up journey. He offers her salvation. She is so happy and excited that she tells the whole town – her whole world – everything she can about Jesus and the personal way He connected with her.

Comparison to the Spiritual Kingdom: Talking to her at all was significantly outside of acceptable behavior in that culture. Yet, Jesus doesn't care about culture, He only cares to love this woman by offering her salvation. Lesson: God & Jesus look beyond culture and love all individuals.

Moral comparison to the Christian lifestyle: We are to look beyond popular culture and reach out to individuals and love them regardless of their past sins.

Comparison to my personal journey: At this point in my life, the Lord had recently prompted me to start writing and speaking. There were no specific instructions after that. I had been feeling a little lost in the fog, honestly; moving toward something I couldn't see or understand on blind faith.

I used my comparison tool and thought, well, how does my journey compare to the woman at the well? She was a lost woman who connected intimately with God and then shouted that news for everyone to hear. The Holy Spirit spoke to my heart, saying, "Ginny, you were once a lost young woman and now you have joyfully been intimately been acquainted with the Lord. I want you to communicate your excitement and joy to the whole world. You are the woman at the well."

This may sound arrogant, but until that day, I had always identified with Jesus in that story. Perhaps it was my pride in never having been divorced that had blurred my vision. I identified with the calling Jesus gave His disciples (to go out and love everyone and make many disciples), but I never once stopped to identify with the woman. The most obvious, gender specific comparison.

On top of that, she is the person drumming up new disciples by telling the world about Jesus. Yet, ultimately, it is when the town comes to know Jesus for themselves that they truly believe, but it is the woman at the well who tells her story and points to Jesus.

This was a revelation to me. God had suddenly put into perspective a personal calling on my life. But, I still did not know what God wanted me to say through my speaking and my writing. That is, until I looked at this story through the filter of the serenity prayer.

What did the woman have to accept? Her past, her sins, her belief that Jesus is the savior.

What did the woman have the power and courage to change? She broke free of her shame of her past. She had the courage to tell her story to anyone who would listen. She didn't have to think of clever things to say to persuade people. She had to speak out her experiences, and that included Jesus.

And there was my path ahead of me. Speaking out my experience and pointing to Jesus.

It is no coincidence that Jesus answered almost every question with a parable or metaphor. He was pointing to the fact that He has made the answers available to us if we know how to compare our lives to the wisdom we find in His word and kingdom.

There are numerous accountings of murderers and adulterers and thieves who are beloved by God and given a place in His love story. He's telling you, that all are welcome, no matter what they've done.

Seven – Seek Godly Counsel.

Ecclesiastes says there is nothing new under the sun.

Well, I don't believe that to be true in the literal sense. Every new baby is another unique creation, brand new under the sun. God is a master creative innovator and He is constantly writing new stories and creating new and personal ways to connect with us.

However, generally speaking, human behavior is quite predictable. We will inevitably fear our future. We will inevitably act instinctively out of that fear. We will inevitably hurt another person physically and/or emotionally despite our best intentions. Our teenage years will be rebellious in certain ways as we struggle to find our personal identity. We will always need food and water to sustain our physical health. We will always need connection and love to be emotionally healthy.

These are just some of the "general truths" that will always remain under the sun. Some of the timeless general truths we learn at a very early age, and others take us much longer to understand. For those more complex truths we can look to our elders for Godly council.

Do not accept the counsel of just anyone. Look at their lives to see how they have lived. Actions are much more revealing than words. Make sure there has been good fruit that has come from their lives. Look for confirmation that they have practiced what they've preached and that they've preached from the word of God about the heart of God.

These mentors will guide us in comparing our experiences not only to their lives, but also to Bible stories, the lives of other men and women so that you may understand where your path may be leading you – whether it's good news or bad.

Asking for help in this way does not show your failings. Your only failing would be to rely upon your own understanding alone.

"Where there is no guidance the people fall, but in abundance of counselors there is victory."
Proverbs 11:14 (ESV)

At some point you've probably thought your story is exempt from the statistics you've heard. The horrible things that happen to *other* people will *never* happen to you. But let me tell you, there are consequences for your actions and all the good intentions you ever had cannot save you from those consequences.

Aggressive, fast driving will kill you more readily.

Smoking just one cigarette per day can get you addicted. Occasionally watching porn will have an effect on your marriage.

These are some not so happy negative truths that I pray you will never need to learn the hard way. Listening to Godly counsel can lead you out of a whole heap of trouble for years to come.

Eight – Act.

If wisdom comes from our personal experiences, then ultimately it is necessary to experience new things to gain wisdom. It doesn't matter if they are painful things, fun things, uncomfortable things, all experiences can provide wisdom.

If you had always stayed within your comfort zone you would be no more useful than a small baby. At some point you had to sit down and learn for school grades; even though you were scared to take tests, you took them. Later you had to step out and have a job interview to pay the bills. Inevitably your hope for your future outweighed your fears.

You may have failed a few tests, or gotten fired from your job. These were hard things to experience because they were outside your comfort zone. But you learned from each one of those experiences. And you take that wisdom forward with you into your next set of experiences.

Eventually we all have to take a leap of faith and hope for the best. Otherwise, a stagnant life will leave you with regrets and "what ifs" circling around in your mind.

Nine – Observe the Effects.

The scientific method is the standard approach to deduction in order to learn things that are physically testable. The most important part of the scientific method is observation. If you perform an experiment and never bother to observe the results, the exercise is fruitless.

Regularly reflect on your decisions in order to observe the effects of your actions.

You could honestly look at your life as one big experiment! Granted, it's not going to be scientific, but it is a sort of experiment. Fair warning though, observing your actions and how other people react is a past time that could consume you, so try not to take the experiment too seriously.

The important part is that you recognize the consequences of your actions – good or bad – and learn to repeat the actions that yield positive results.

Make sure to forgive yourself and others along the way when the experiment goes south. Hold tightly to the good memories. Let the bad memories hang loosely around you, and only for the purpose of remembering the lesson you learned.

Ten - Help Others.

Once you have gained wisdom, carefully bestow that wisdom to others. In doing so, you will remind yourself of what you already know.

There have been numerous occasions when I've been asked to provide wisdom or shed light on a specific problem, and as I give guidance realize I should be taking my own advice in my own life.

Remember, there is nothing new under the sun (Ecclesiastes 1:9). Drama repeats itself and you will need the same wisdom you dole out time and time again.

Prayer

Heavenly Father,
I recognize that my knowledge and experience are miniscule compared to Your vast wisdom. Help me to seek Your will as I make decisions. Reveal Your wisdom as I reflect on my options. I pray my actions will glorify Your name and strengthen Your kingdom.
In Jesus' name, Amen.

10

AMEN
What happens now?

"If you believe, you will receive whatever you ask for in prayer."

Matthew 21:22

Even though we may end our requests with the word amen, do not be fooled into thinking this is the end of our prayer. Not at all. Amen marks the beginning of our prayer in action.

The literal translation of amen is "so be it" or "let it be so." In this way, amen is a declaration of faith. It is a declaration that our requests have been heard and God is putting all requests into motion that are for our good.

By declaring amen in Jesus' name, we are declaring our confirmation of trust in His promises. Our prayers become active forces in God's kingdom.

We can rest knowing He will give us the full life He promised. He is working in us – helping us to release the physical cares of this world and grab ahold of the spiritual freedom He offers. Each Serenity Prayer brings us closer to loving with our whole heart, forgiving with every breath, and thanking God for every moment of this unpredictable, messy life. It means we are trading in worry for trust, anger for love, and surrender for serenity.

Yet, be patient. The positive effects of this practice will not come over night. Changing your behavior and thought patterns will not happen immediately. Drama takes time to untangle – both within us and with others. The Lord will guide us and help us, but he does not do the work for us. We must put forth our own effort as well. Over time, with consistent commitment to the Serenity Prayer principles you will see your life transform, fulfilling God's promises.

Recruit Supporters.

In addition to walking closely with the Lord, we need to surround ourselves with a support system of people who allow us to be our authentic selves. On our own, we are limited, but with help from the Lord and others we can accomplish far more.

Even Jesus had twelve disciples. He could not run His ministry on His own. He needed help managing money and crowds and food distribution and food collection (12 baskets of leftovers from just a few loaves and fishes!).

As a coach and a sponsor, I have seen women suffering from extreme fear and exhaustion transform into women exhilarated by confidence and freedom. It was the power of God, but it was only possible because they reached out for help.

Contrary to what you've been told, needing help is not a weakness – it is a universal reality. Pride tells us we should be enough, but faith tells us our brokenness is enough. Needing help is not what makes us weak; rather it is denying our need that weakens us.

There are counselors, coaches, mentors, support groups, 12-step programs, family and friends that may have a powerful role to play in your story. By working with a coach, you will reach your goals 3 times faster. Imagine if a coach was only the beginning. How quickly would your journey change by reaching out to as many support systems as you actually need?

To live is to experience adventure.

In the days to come, sin will be present and its drama will echo. Injustice will befall you. Emotions will sway from high to low and back to high. This is all part of your great adventure. This is what it means to be alive.

No matter what, continue applying these principles and you'll find it easier to identify where drama begins. Drama's impact will be less and less as you learn to nip it in the bud. You'll even prepare yourself to face vulnerability before it starts.

Keep trusting in the Lord above all else, for this is the cornerstone of peace.

"The Lord bless you and keep you; the Lord make his face shine on you and be gracious to you; the Lord turn his face toward you and give you peace."

Numbers 6:24-26

About the Author

Ginny Priz is a Certified Christian Life Coach and Speaker. She is also creator of the Ditch the D.R.A.M.A. audio series, and a weekly Serenity video blog. Being born without a full right arm was the blessing that gave her faith in God's plan for her life. Plus, her prosthetic comes in handy when making one-arm-liners!

After college, she spent a decade struggling with anxiety, codependency, and addiction. Finally, Ginny fully trusted God guide her journey. It was a decision that completely transformed her life to one of joy and freedom. Today, she has a passion for sharing this transformational power to help others.

Ginny's personal mission is to help women break free of fear and emotions holding them back from living in freedom with Christ so that they can achieve their dreams and walk in God's will for their lives.

One of her greatest honors has been to serve as a teacher and sponsor through the Celebrate Recovery program. When she is not working or catching up with friends, Ginny enjoys watching science-fiction movies, hiking, and finding new ways to use her prosthetic as a punch line.

To learn more about her speaking and coaching services you can visit her online at:

www.serenityjourneyministries.com.
www.ditchthedrama.net.
Facebook: www.facebook.com/ginnypriz
Twitter: www.twitter.com/ginnypriz

https://www.facebook.com/groups/SerenityJourney
This is a safe place where women can receive encouragement and ask for prayer amongst fellow Serenity Seekers.

60837212R00091

Made in the USA
Middletown, DE
16 August 2019